1335

BANKING COMPUTER STYLE

*The Impact of Computers on Small
and Medium-Sized Banks*

JAMES A. VAUGHAN
Associate Professor of
Business Administration and Psychology

AVNER M. PORAT
Assistant Professor of Business Administration

Management Research Center
College of Business Administration
The University of Rochester

With Contribution By John A. Haas

PRENTICE-HALL, INC., Englewood Cliffs, New Jersey

C-13-055491-X
P-13-055483-9
Library of Congress Catalog Card Number: 79-94638

Current printing (last digit)

10 9 8 7 6 5 4 3 2 1

PRENTICE-HALL INTERNATIONAL, INC., *London*
PRENTICE-HALL OF AUSTRALIA PTY. LTD., *Sydney*
PRENTICE-HALL OF CANADA, LTD., *Toronto*
PRENTICE-HALL OF INDIA PRIVATE LTD., *New Delhi*
PRENTICE-HALL OF JAPAN, INC., *Tokyo*

Foreword

In recent years many small and medium-sized commercial banks have followed the lead of larger banks and acquired or gained access to computer facilities, and they have done so through a variety of arrangements. The process has not always been a smooth or well-planned one. Costs, staffing problems and the need for organizational changes have frequently exceeded expectations. Even where computerization has been effected smoothly, the process has largely been restricted to check clearing and relatively routine servicing operations. Very few banks have thus far tapped much of the computer potential for effecting the decision-making process.

In this study, James A. Vaughan and Avner M. Porat examine the problems associated with the acquisition of computer facilities by small and medium-sized banks, focusing on the managerial and operational problems that have occurred during the early years of computerization by these banks. The authors' observations, analyses, and recommendations should be of considerable interest and value to banks planning to acquire computer facilities as well as those that have already done so.

The research for this study was financed jointly by the FDIC and the Graduate school of Business Administration at the University of Pittsburgh. The views expressed are those of the authors and do not necessarily reflect official views of the FDIC.

K. A. Randall
Chairman

June 10, 1969

Acknowledgement.

The authors wish to express their appreciation to all those in F.D.I.C. who very graciously contributed time and ideas to this research project. Dr. Frederick S. Hammer, Dr. Paul Horvitz, Mr. Jack E. Edington and Mr. Clayton A. Miller were especially helpful throughout the study.

We are likewise indebted to the bank managers who participated in this research. Without exception, they welcomed us into their banks and were eager to contribute their experience and thinking to the study.

Finally, thanks are due to our secretary at The Management Research Center, Mrs. Retta Holdorf, who was patient and helpful through many drafts of the manuscript.

J.A.V.
A.M.P.

Contents

Chapter 1

*The Nature
of Automation in Banking   6*

Chapter 2

Chapter 3

Chapter 4

Chapter 5

Introduction

Twelve to fifteen years ago a statement such as "computers are here to stay" brought howls of protest from those who were skeptical of their long-run utility. Today virtually no one questions the continued existence of computers as a significant factor in organizational life. Nowhere is this more true than in the banking industry. Nevertheless, there are still many unanswered questions regarding the impact to date of computers on organizations and their members and the role they will play in the future.

This book is an attempt to shed some light on these issues. It is based primarily on a 1967 study sponsored by the Federal Deposit Insurance Corporation. There were two major goals of the study. The first was to define as precisely as possible the changes in banking organizations which are associated with the introduction of computers; the second, to provide some normative statements based on the findings as to how commercial banks, especially the small to medium-sized ones, should handle the process of automating.

Data collection was organized into five areas:

1. The history of computer services in the bank, including the reasons for considering Electronic Data Processing (EDP), the processes used

to arrive at the first decision to accept or reject the use of EDP services, the strategies used to execute the decision, the conversion period, and future plans for the use of EDP.

2. The impact of the computer on the flow and content of information within the bank, including changes in reports and use of information by the various officers in the bank.

3. The effects of computer usage on specific banking jobs, including the behavior of individuals performing the jobs, the way individuals believe they spend their time at work, how they believe they should be spending their time, and specific changes that occurred as a result of the computer.

4. The attitudes of bank personnel toward use of the computer and behavioral manifestations of these attitudes, including causes for the development of various attitudes, their impact on the development and use of EDP in the bank, and ways to avoid negative reactions and take advantage of positive ones.

5. The effects of computer usage on organizational structure, including changes in the size of departments, the reporting relations between departments, and changes in the decision-making structure.

The Study Methods

The main study population included 57 commercial banks, ranging in size from $10 to $50 million in deposits. (Some additional data were utilized from a prior study in a large metropolitan bank.) The 57 banks were selected, using a modified random sampling technique, from a list of over 300 banks in the desired size range. The modification employed was a deliberate attempt to approximate a representative sample with regard to geographic distribution of the subject banks. The locations of the participating banks represent all major parts of the U.S. mainland. (See Appendix A.) The banks were divided into three major groups and six subgroups based on the type of automation used by the bank, as shown in Table 1.

Three methods of data collection were utilized:

1. *Study of written records.* The two main types of written records used were (a) information supplied by the FDIC and (b) records maintained by the banks.

   To the disappointment of the authors, most banks had few written records pertaining to the process of deciding whether or not to acquire EDP services, the conversion period, or the subsequent development.

2. *Field interviews.* All 57 participating banks were visited by the

Table 1

FORM OF AUTOMATION USED BY PARTICIPATING BANKS

		No. of banks
I.	Use computer on-premises	18
II.	Use computer off-premises	
	Correspondent bank 12	
	Independent service bureau 7	
	Holding company computer center 7	
	Joint venture center 5	
	—	31
III.	Do not use computer services at present	
	Definite plans for using computer 4	
	No definite plans for using computer 4	
	—	8
	Total	57

researchers. In each, four to eight interviews, each lasting 45 minutes to 2 hours, were conducted with the top officers and with other key people associated with EDP operations. A semi-structured interview schedule was employed, allowing the interview to be adjusted according to the interviewee's position in the bank. That is, while the interviews generally covered all of the five areas of investigation described above, those areas most relevant to the person being interviewed were explored in greater depth.

3. *Questionnaires.* Following the visit to each bank, two questionnaires were mailed to every officer and supervisor in the bank, regardless of whether or not they had been interviewed. (Questionnaires were not sent to those 8 banks not using computers at the time.) The questionnaires were returned unsigned so that anonymity of the respondents was assured.

The major questionnaire consisted of two parts: the first asked for biographical and job-related information; the second, for attitudes on a series of issues related to the computer and its effect on the organization.

The second questionnaire also consisted of two parts. The first asked for managers' estimates of their *actual* allocation of time among several broad classes of activities and for their *preferred* time allocations for the same activities. The second asked for the managers' estimates of their *actual* and *preferred* time allocations for contact with other persons or sources of information within the organization. (Both questionnaires are included in Appendix B.)

A total of 710 questionnaires were mailed, of which 438 (61.7 per cent) usable returns were received and included in the analysis. The percentages of usable questionnaires returned by banks are given in Table 2.

Table 2

RESPONSES TO THE QUESTIONNAIRE

Per cent of useable returns	*No. of banks*
100 per cent	4
67 to 99 per cent	20
34 to 66 per cent	19
1 to 33 per cent	5
No returns	1*
Total	49

*Seven questionnaires were mailed to this bank.

The questionnaire data were analyzed by using as independent variables for the purpose of comparing the attitudinal responses the type of automation arrangement and selected "objective" items, such as length of EDP experience, size of deposits, number of total staff and departmental identification. The results are reported and discussed in the body of this book.

Plan of the Book

Chapter 1 describes the nature of the changes which have occurred in the banking industry over the last two decades and the resulting pressures for banks to automate. In particular, the development of the "new-look" marketing orientation is discussed along with a brief historical account of the use of EDP. Chapter 2 describes the alternative forms of automation available to banks today and discusses advantages and disadvantages of each form.

Chapter 3 relates the manner in which decisions to automate have been made in the past and suggests some techniques for improving the decision-making process. It concentrates on the five phases of the feasibility study, which is seen as an absolute necessity. Chapter 4 discusses the importance of planning for conversion and relates some of the problems which can be anticipated and perhaps avoided or minimized. Human resistance to change has generally been a bigger problem than the technical aspects of conversion; consequently, attention is focused on the overall issues of change rather than on specific technical problems. Chapter 5 describes the impact of computers on the information system and ultimately the structure of the organization. It was found that changes in the former have occurred much more rapidly than changes in the latter. Chapter 6 considers the effects of computers on banking jobs in terms of changes in numbers of jobs as well as skill requirements. Special attention is given to the position of the new breed of computer experts in the industry. Chapter 7 discusses the training problems relating to the introduction of computers and suggests some techniques for dealing with them. Finally, Chapter 8 describes the challenges a bank faces in maintaining its automation program and in participating in future developments. A case is made for the early entry into *feasible* applications which have long-term potential for the total automation program.

Chapter 1

The Nature
of Automation in Banking

The banking industry has been an active participant in a major development in American business, namely, the computer revolution. The adoption of the computer, or more generally, Electronic Data Processing (EDP) in banking is on the one hand closely related to the changes in the structure and nature of operations of the banking industry itself, and on the other, to the emergence of the computer as a significant organizational tool. This chapter will review both trends and then examine the specific reasons why individual banks become interested in EDP.

1.1 The Expansion of Banking Services

The financial system in the United States, of which the commercial banks are a major segment, changes constantly with the appearance of new financial institutions and the evolution of existing institutions. Today, in addition to competition from mutual savings banks, the commercial bank faces stiff competition from a variety of financial institutions, including Credit Unions, Savings and Loan Associations, Personal Finance Companies, Sales Finance Companies, Industrial Loan Companies and Money Order Companies.

Bankers have been cautioned that unless they adapt to change quickly and effectively they will inevitably lose their dominant position in the market. To some extent this happened to commercial banks during the late fifties and early sixties, as indicated below.

> "At the opening of the twentieth century, commercial banks were, by a very wide margin, the leading financial institutions in the United States. Whether measured by size or by the qualitative importance of the financial services they rendered, they were considerably more important than all other types of financial institutions combined. Since that time, commercial banks have grown, but they have not grown as rapidly as other financial institutions. Commercial banks have lost somewhat in the competitive race. A number of other types of financial institutions are now enjoying a considerably more rapid rate of growth." (Robinson, 1962, pp. 21-22.)

Since the time of these observations, however, it is our impression that the banking industry has regained much of the ground it had lost. An important reason for the increase in the supply of "financial-banking" services has been the drastic change in the demand for banking services. From an *exclusive* institution for the rich members of the community and business world, the commercial bank has changed to a *public* institution catering to all segments of society. This is especially true of the smaller bank, which found it difficult to compete effectively with the larger banks for the big business accounts and thus had to concentrate on the smaller accounts. At the same time, the industry has experienced an increase in the sophistication of its customers— both individuals and corporate managers. The fact that today's financial customers can and do shop for services has put considerable pressure on the banking industry to increase and improve its services at all levels. (Yavitz, 1967.)

Stiffer competition and the demand for more and better banking services have caused considerable growth in several areas. While in the last 20 years there was almost no change (actually a slight decline) in the number of commercial banks operating in the United States, the number of bank offices increased by 72 per cent. (See Table 1.1.) This was accompanied by an increase of 166 per cent in the size of banking assets. To handle this growth, the industry more than doubled the number of banking employees within the same period of time.

Changes have occurred in almost all areas of banking services. For example, in the deposits area, commercial banks have traditionally concentrated on *demand* deposits as their main source of funds, whereas, prior to the 1960's, non-banking institutions generally enjoyed a distinct advantage over commercial banks in their ability to attract *time* deposits by being permitted to pay higher interest rates. As late as 1950, time deposits accounted for only 27 per cent of the total deposits in commercial banks. In 1955 this trend started to change and by 1967, due to increased efforts in attracting time deposits, the proportion had risen to 47 per cent of total

Table 1.1

THE DEVELOPMENT OF THE BANKING INDUSTRY 1947-67

Year	No. banks	No. bank offices	Size of bank assets (millions)	No. employ.	Growth since 1947 (in percentages)			
					Banks	Offices	Assets size	Employ.
1967	13,762	31,860	415,436	850	−3.3	72.5	165.8	106.8
1962	13,439	25,930	298,196	713	−5.6	40.4	98.8	73.7
1957	13,607	21,969	224,020	603	−4.4	18.9	43.3	46.7
1952	14,088	19,675	189,597	512	−1.2	6.5	21.3	24.6
1947	14,234	18,471	156,293	411	−	−	−	−

Source: FDIC Annual Reports, 1947-67.

deposits. The need to pay interest on the time accounts increased the banks' expenses, requiring them to seek new areas of revenues with higher return on investment. In the demand deposits area itself, customers can now open a large variety of accounts such as "Thrifty," "Special," and "Regular." Similar changes have occurred in the loan area, where a variety of plans are now available for purposes that were out of the question 20 years ago.

In addition to changes and expansion in the conventional banking functions, the "full service banks," especially the larger ones, are becoming fully involved in such new services as credit cards, travel, commercial billing, payroll, and account reconciliation, to mention a few. With the emergence of these new services and the rapid expansion of the number of banking offices, a new image for banking has been created. Instead of sitting back and waiting for customers to come to them, banks have begun to go to the customers. And instead of waiting for customers to ask for their needs to be met with certain services, banks have begun to anticipate and to tell customers what their needs are.

Probably the best way to characterize the change we are describing is to say that banks have become marketing-oriented. As one banker described the situation, with tongue in cheek, bankers "discovered" marketing in the mid-1950's. For some the change has been a conscious, deliberate one; for others it has been more of an evolutionary process. The extent to which individual banks have evidenced this transformation varies, of course. However, the trend is now quite obvious, and most banks are making a concerted effort to shed their cloaks of ultra-conservatism and to take on new service-oriented images.

This change in marketing philosophy has been felt throughout the entire bank, especially at the branch level. The following comments of one branch manager constitute a good summary of the impact of the new orientation.

> "The retail bank concept with all the new innovations derived from EDP has changed the bank manager's position primarily into that of a sales manager. Responsibilities for clean operations and sound lending practices are his responsibility, but second to the sales goal necessary to reach satisfactory quotas. The clerical staff has become a selling staff, and sales emphasis has required a complete change in hiring and training practices." (Porat and Vaughan, 1967a.)

This may, in fact, be an overstatement of an individual situation, but it certainly conveys the flavor of the transformation. These developments could not have taken place in most cases without considerable improvements in the methods of operation and the help of advanced equipment, primarily the computer.

1.2 Development of Automation in Banking

Over the last 15 years the computer, or more generally, Electronic Data Processing (EDP), has become an accepted tool in many organizations and has had a considerable impact on the organizational environment and its members. From 1955-66 the number of computers installed in business and government organizations increased from less than 100 to 28,500. Industry projections indicate that by 1970 there will be 60,000 computers (valued at $18 billion) in use. (Myers, 1967, p. 1.)

The first commercial computer in the United States, UNIVAC-1, became operative in 1953 at the Bureau of Census; by the end of 1954 the first privately-used unit was delivered by Remington Rand to the General Electric Company. In late 1955, International Business Machines introduced its Model 650. UNIVAC and the Model 650 became the first commercially available computers and marked the beginning of the computer era. At about the same time at least two banks, the Bank of America and the First National City Bank of New York, were experimenting with computer processing, and the Banks Management Commission of the American Bankers Association began to investigate the possibility of a nationwide system for standardized checks. When the ABA issued its "Check Standards Under the Common Machine Language" at the end of 1960, the early pioneers among the large banks and the computer companies abandoned their independent processing systems; computer processing of demand deposits was advanced from the individual bank level to an industrywide system. (Yavitz, 1967, Ch. 2.)

Still, EDP developments within the banking industry were, until the mid-1960's, confined mainly to the large banks with deposits of over $100 million. An industry survey suggested that by the end of 1966 only 20 per cent of the banks with less than $100 million in deposits were using any type of computer services, on- or off-premises (American Banking Association, 1966). The same study predicted that by the end of 1971, 45 per cent of the banks in this size category would be using some type of computer service. In total, the study anticipated that between 1967-71 at least 3,200 additional banks will start to use computers, bringing the total to 55 per cent of all commercial banks and accounting for over 90 per cent of total deposits.

There are several reasons why small to medium-sized banks were slow in adopting the use of computers. In the beginning, the main obstacle was the hardware—the computer itself. Computer manufacturers concentrated on the large corporations and were slow in introducing equipment which could replace the conventional bookkeeping equipment and compete effectively with the electronic bookkeeping machines (usually known as "tronics"). There existed a notion among top management in smaller banks that the computer was only for larger banks and too expensive an investment for the smaller banks to handle. The equipment manufacturers, who were busy supplying their larger customers with complex systems, did little to discourage this notion. As late as the early 1960's this part of the computer market was still a seller's market such that the small to medium-sized banks had to seek out computer suppliers, rather than vice versa.

In addition to the lack of equipment, there existed almost a complete lack of knowledge about what the computer could and should do for banks. The larger banks could afford to hire special staffs to plan and execute the introduction of EDP into the organization and to develop the software needed for the operation. The smaller banks were unable or unwilling to acquire such specialists. It was not until the mid-1960's, when the manufacturers started in earnest to pursue the market of the small to medium-sized banks, that information about EDP started to become readily available to those organizations.

This knowledge gap was noted in 1966 by George W. Mitchell, member of the Board of Governors of the Federal Reserve System, in a speech before a national bankers' convention devoted to automation:

> "For bankers these [EDP] handling methods are novel. They are scientific developments conceived and perfected completely outside of the banking industry. They do not employ skills or expertise common to banking; indeed, they have an almost alchemistic aura in contrast to the image or reality of banking as we know it."

A complete re-orientation of management's thinking plus increasing operational and competitive pressures had to occur before the idea of computer use in small business could be accepted by the people running the bank.

1.3 The Pressure to Automate

For the individual bank, the pressure to automate usually results from one of two causes: the bank may be experiencing an overload in the operations area which traditional bookkeeping equipment cannot handle; or it may be looking toward future developments in the banking industry with an eye towards improving its competitive position. The first can be defined as a short-term cue which mainly falls under the heading of operational pressure, while the second can be defined as a long-term cue falling under the heading of policy planning.

1.3.1 Operational Problems

One of the most critical problem areas has been the processing of demand deposits. The number of checks written annually has risen from 5.3 billion in 1945 to just under 12.7 billion in 1960, to 17 billion in 1965 and is expected, by conservative estimates, to be in excess of 22.7 billion per year in 1970. (See Table 1.2.) Two trends account for this tremendous rise in the number of checks written. The first is an increase in the number of checks written per account (up 52 per cent from 1945-64). For example, the turnover of deposits in New York City banks increased from 25 times per annum in 1946 to 78 times per annum in 1962. (Nadler, 1964, p. 53.) The second is the 100 per cent increase in the number of demand deposit accounts between 1945-64. The latter is expected to increase by another 30 per cent by 1975. Because each check passes through 2-1/3 banks on the average, and may be handled up to 20 times before being returned to the person who wrote it, paper work has threatened to flood the banks. (Wiener, 1962, p. 990.)

As a result:

"The check-processing department has emerged in the past 20 years as the largest department in the average bank in terms of personnel and equipment investment costs. Encoders, proof machines, sorters, and computer systems, together with expensive staffs to man them, comprise the major investment in dollars and talent by the banking industry to stay abreast of the flood of checks today. There are only a few banks in the country today where the 'factory' operation of check

processing is not a significant concern for bank management."
(Anderson, 1966, p. 67.)

Table 1.2

NUMBER OF ACCOUNTS AND CHECKS IN DEMAND DEPOSITS (Selected Years)

Year	No. of demand deposits accounts (millions)	Total number of checks (billions)	No. of checks cleared per account per month
1975*	92.0	29.0	263
1970*	78.0	22.7	242
1965	70.9	16.0	188
1955	52.2	9.5	152
1945	35.6	5.3	124

*Forecast.
Source: 1945-65: Anderson (et al) p. 68-69.
        1970-75: Wiener, (1962).

The increase in paper work has also been felt in other areas of banking:

"Changes in investment and loan policies between 1950 and 1960
also caused shifts from activities requiring relatively little processing to
those requiring a great deal. For example, investments in bonds, which
require little handling by bank employees, became much less important
in relation to loans, which require much more paper work. Consumer
installment loans, which require the most handling, more than doubled
in volume during the period." (Wiener, 1962, p. 990.)

So it is not surprising that while the floor officers were pursuing new sources
of income and fighting increasing competition, operation officers were
seeking new methods, techniques and equipment that would relieve the data
processing pressures.

In 34 of the 49 automated banks we visited, top management stated that
operational problems were the chief reasons for seriously considering
automation. (See Table 1.3.) Of the remaining 15 banks, 5 were new banks
which decided to automate from the day of opening. The decision-makers in
these new ventures were men with banking experience, and to them the
decision to automate was relatively clear-cut. They saw the off-premises
computer service as a way to avoid a large initial investment in their own
equipment and viewed EDP as the only long-run solution to a bank's data
processing needs. Not having to weigh the cost of a conversion, their decision
was relatively easy.

Table 1.3

THE MAJOR REASONS GIVEN FOR CONSIDERING EDP[1]

Reasons	No. of banks mentioning the reason as the major influence
Operational pressures—	
1. Maintaining the system:	
Personnel problems in the bookkeeping department	14
Maintaining bookkeeping machines	8
2. Expanding volume of operations:	
Need to accommodate increasing volume	11
Need to maintain or reduce costs	7
3. Unsatisfactory output:	
Errors in reports and statements	9
Delays in processing work	4
Need for system change	2
Other reasons—	
Observation of effective automation programs in other banks	7
Felt need to meet competition	7
Desire to produce additional revenues	2
New bank minimizing investment	5
Instructions to automate from owners	6

[1] Some banks gave more than one major reason.

The importance of operational pressures in initiating the automation processes was confirmed in the 1966 ABA survey by questioning banks which were not planning to use EDP services in the foreseeable future. Their most important reason for *not* automating, given by nearly 60 per cent of the total banks in the ABA survey and 50 per cent of the $10-50 million banks, was that the present system of bookkeeping and operation was adequate for the bank. One-third of the small banks surveyed responded that they had adopted a "wait and see" policy, while 16 per cent of these banks frankly stated that they believed their banks to be too small for computer processing. In other words, the majority of the respondents decided not to use EDP services mainly because they did not feel the immediate pressure to do so or were waiting for further developments, rather than because they felt EDP was not suitable or feasible for their operations.

Table 1.4

REASONS GIVEN BY BANKERS FOR NOT USING OR PLANNING TO USE
EDP SERVICES

	All banks N=1642		Bank size $10-$49 million N=322	
	No.	*Per cent*	*No.*	*Per cent*
Present system is adequate	967	59.4	162	50.3
Present equipment is still being amortized	336	20.4	84	26.1
Applications in our bank are too small for computer processing	565	34.4	52	16.2
No computer facilities are available to us within a reasonable distance	253	15.4	39	12.1
We have adopted a "wait and see" attitude	457	27.8	107	33.2
A study indicated that a computer service was not available at this time	210	12.8	67	20.8
No response	71	4.3	22	13.9

Source: ABA Automation Survey, 1966.

The specific operational pressures mentioned in the banks we studied fell into three major categories: personnel, equipment and unsatisfactory operations. As we noted above, banks currently employ more than twice as many people as they did in 1947. During the same 20-year period, employment in all industries combined increased only 49.1 per cent. The increases become even more significant if we separate the categories of supervisory and non-supervisory employees (Figure 1.1). Since 1958 (the first year that the Department of Labor made this distinction) the number of supervisory people in banks increased a staggering 64.6 per cent, compared to a 35.0 per cent increase for non-supervisory employees. The relatively greater increase in the number of supervisory personnel is probably a result of (1) increased sophistication of banking operations and (2) extensive use of the computer for work which was previously done by non-supervisory employees. In other words, without the computer, the number of non-supervisory banking employees could have been expected to rise considerably faster.

Many banks reported that it was becoming increasingly difficult to recruit, train and keep competent personnel in the bookkeeping department. Overtime was commonplace, as was a relatively high rate of turnover. The turnover problem was further complicated by the fact that traditionally the majority of workers in the bookkeeping departments were women, who found it more difficult to adjust to long periods of overtime work.

FIGURE 1.1 ANNUAL PERCENTAGE INCREASE OF SUPERVISORY AND NON-SUPERVISORY EMPLOYEES IN BANKING COMPARED WITH ALL INDUSTRIES SINCE 1958

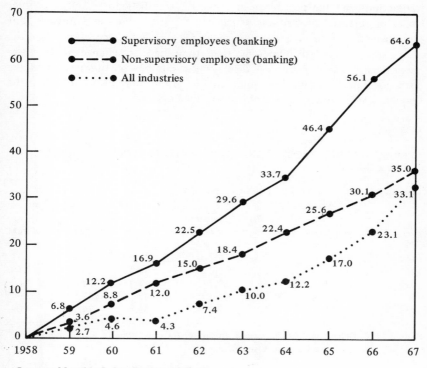

Source: Monthly Labor Review 1959-67.

In addition, some banks found themselves in a much tougher job market than in the past so that they were forced to pay more money for people they did not expect to remain with the bank for any length of time. Table 1.5 shows the continuous increase in average weekly gross earning of non-supervisory banking workers since 1947.

The second significant variable in maintaining the system was machinery. Many banks reported their posting machines to be as temperamental as some of the people operating them. In addition, as machines become obsolete, new machines are not always readily available. The same manufacturers that were pushing the "tronics" in previous years have put their sales effort into selling computers, and they have discouraged use of other bookkeeping equipment.

The ever increasing volume of operations accompanied by manpower and equipment problems increased the incidence of errors in the bookkeeping output and caused considerable delays in completing the output. For years bankers have strived to maintain a 24-hour cycle of operations, i.e., yesterday's transactions would be posted by the opening of today's business day. Their goal has been to avoid a slowdown in execution of customers' transactions and the possibility of losing the dissatisfied customers to other banks or financial institutions which could provide improved services. For some banks the pressures in maintaining such a cycle became so great and the errors and delays so numerous that they had to change their entire operational system. Table 1.3 displays the number of times each of the operational problems was mentioned by one of the study banks, as well as the frequency with which other problems were mentioned.

Table 1.5

AVERAGE WEEKLY GROSS EARNINGS OF NON-SUPERVISORY WORKERS IN BANKING

			No. of employees per		
Year	Average gross earnings	Per cent increase since 1947	Bank	Banking office	Assets
1947	37.76	—	28.9	22.3	2.41
1952	50.23	33.0	36.3	26.0	2.70
1957	61.44	62.7	44.3	27.4	2.69
1962	72.17	91.1	52.1	27.5	2.39
1967	86.44	129.8	61.8	26.7	2.04

Source: U.S. Department of Commerce, Business Statistics, Biennial Supplement to Survey of Current Business.

1.3.2 Policy Planning

Among the non-operational reasons for automating, the most significant given were those resulting from the general effects of EDP developments in banking. That is, some bank officers were very favorably impressed after observing successful EDP operations in other banks, and some felt a strong need to get started in an automation program in order to prepare themselves to meet the competition from other banks in the future—especially in the area of non-banking services.[1]

---

[1] It is our opinion that even though these were given as chief reasons, they would not have been sufficient reasons had the banks in question not also been experiencing some operational problems.

Several years ago larger banks started to engage in a continuous activity of developing new types of services for old and new customers to supplement the revenues from traditional banking services. But even today many smaller banks hesitate to move towards adopting these new services. In only two of the banks studied did the decision seem to be heavily influenced by the desire to expand services or to use the computer as a revenue-producing instrument. In both cases, as well as in several banks now engaged in automated customer services, management felt that the computer helped to increase revenues. However, the contribution to profits is difficult to estimate due to the lack of cost accounting systems and is doubtful at best.

1.4 Summary

Both of the above factors—the success of some banks in utilizing computers and the perceived attractiveness of offering new services via computers—have combined to cause many bankers to feel a great urgency to get on the computer bandwagon immediately. As a consequence, during the last five years many banks have undertaken automation programs which are not really appropriate to their needs. No bank should feel compelled to automate or to be left behind competitively. It is more important to consider carefully when and how the bank will enter the field of automation. The following chapter presents some alternative forms of automation which are now available.

Chapter 2

Alternate Forms
of Automation Available

Once the pressure to change the operations system has been recognized and management begins to examine the possibility of using EDP in the bank, it must decide which of the various types of arrangements will be most suitable for the bank. The present chapter will describe five alternative types of automation arrangements and illustrate the issues involved in adopting each of them for the bank.

The forms of EDP available to the small commercial bank can be classified into two major groups. The first is off-premises processing. Under such an arrangement the bank uses the EDP services of a center managed by someone outside the bank, although in the cases of a joint venture or holding company, the bank's management might have a voice in managing the center. The different forms included in off-premises processing are: (1) participating in a joint venture; using (2) a correspondent bank's center, (3) a service bureau computer center or, in special cases, (4) a holding company computer center. The second group is the on-premises arrangement in which the equipment is located on or near the bank's premises and is owned or leased by the bank. Under this arrangement, the EDP department functions as an internal department and is under the direct supervision and control of the bank's management.

Within each of the types or forms of automation described below there are almost an infinite number of individual sub-arrangements which a given bank might take. Examples would be a service bureau owned by the bank as a separate identity, a joint venture monopolized by a single bank, or a combination of using on- and off-premises arrangements. Nevertheless, the discussion will be limited to the five basic types, as the purpose is to indicate the general implications of choosing one type over another. More specifically, the primary focus of the chapter will be to look at the factors which should influence a bank's choice and the impact each type of automation has on the operations of the bank.

Theoretically, all five alternative forms are open to a given bank. In actuality, however, there are usually some compelling reasons for a bank to choose one type over another. For example, for a long time there existed the notion that the small or medium-sized bank could not afford an on-premises computer. To a degree this was supported by figures about the actual types of arrangements used. Out of 1,183 state banks with deposits of less than $100 million supervised by the FDIC and using EDP in 1967, 1,031 (87 per cent) used off-premises EDP and only 152 (13 per cent) had their own on-premises operations. Yet, although the on-premises computer requires considerable commitment, the discussion of this arrangement will note that it should not automatically be eliminated from consideration by the small bank.

Overall, the 1966 ABA study estimated that of the 3,000 banks computerized at that time, 31 per cent used on-premises arrangements, with the remaining banks utilizing off-premises EDP (Table 2.1), again with the majority of larger banks (over $100 million in deposits) using on-premises EDP.

2.1 Off-Premises Arrangements

2.1.1 Using Another Bank's Service

A 1967 survey by the FDIC of supervised state commercial banks with deposits of under $100 million found that of 1,031 banks utilizing off-premises EDP arrangements, 854 (82.8 per cent) were using another bank's computer service. Of the remaining banks, 150 (14.5 per cent) were using service bureau computers, and only 27 banks (2.6 per cent) were participating in joint ventures.

There are several reasons why a bank may decide to use another bank's service. First, the bank planning to automate is not required to have a complete staff which is familiar in detail with computer programming and systems work, although having at least one such person is, of course, desirable. Second, the automating bank benefits from the learning experience of the service provider, while saving money on additional personnel and equipment.

Table 2.1

TYPE OF EDP ARRANGEMENT USED BY BANKS (1966)

Size of deposits ($ millions)	Banks using computer		Type arrangement used (in percentage)	
	Number*	Per cent of total in group	On-premise	Off-premise
Under 10	1166	11.4	3.3	96.7
10-49	1186	39.5	28.6	71.4
50-99	264	78.6	77.3	22.7
100-499	295	95.2	93.6	6.4
500 and over	87	100.0	98.9	1.1
Total	2998	21.4	31.5	68.5

*Projected from responses to the 1966 American Bankers Associates automation questionnaire.

Theoretically then, the conversion is relatively simple. The automating bank uses the programs developed by the service-providing bank and takes advantage of the know-how accumulated. This assumes, of course, that the servicing bank has developed some competence in this area, and furthermore that it has the necessary personnel to provide whatever help the automating bank needs in converting. Herein lies one of the potential drawbacks of using another bank's service. *That is, the system which the servicing bank has developed may not be optimal for the subject bank; yet evidence shows that in most cases the bank providing the service will take the programs which it already has in use and apply them in the new bank without modifications or with only minimal ones. In a real sense then, the ultimate effectiveness of the automation program will depend on the quality of the service purchased rather than on the bank which is automating.

Another reason frequently cited, especially by smaller banks, for choosing a correspondent for their computer services is the long lasting relationship which often exists between the bank and its correspondent. If the officers in the bank have been satisfied with their past relationship with their correspondent, they will be tempted to consult it again in new areas of operations rather than develop new relationships with a service bureau or get involved in the organizational and financial problems of establishing on-premises EDP services (Ankeny, 1967). In cases where the correspondent relationship has been a close one so that there is a real appreciation of the bank's situation, this can be a very significant advantage.

A few study banks indicated they felt some pressure from their correspondent to use their service. In recent years more and more large banks with EDP facilities have launched aggressive drives to solicit the processing business of small banks. Some large banks offer their services to other banks in a radius of up to 300 miles and employ special salesmen whose sole job is to solicit business for the computer department. The transfer of the data to be processed is normally accomplished by car, although a few banks use helicopters or small-plane service. Several banks have been experimenting with the use of remote data stations where data are transmitted to the service center through regular telephone lines. It is expected that within a few years the use of remote data stations will become more feasible regarding cost, and this should eliminate many of the problems of the transportation of documents.

It is not necessary that the bank providing the service be a giant bank or one's correspondent. Two of the banks included in our study, both under $50 million in deposits, have begun providing EDP services for other small banks and in both cases management reports the operation to be successful—in terms of their own profit as well as customer satisfaction.

Two elements of concern were expressed by the study banks regarding the use of another bank's EDP service. First, there was a concern that if their own customers found out they were actually being serviced by another bank they would probably switch banks. The concern was based on the assumption that the customer patronizing the small bank does so because he believes in a specialized personal service that includes the bookkeeping operations. We are unaware of any cases which might support this concern; nevertheless, it exists. A second concern was that it would give the bank providing the service too much privileged information regarding the subject bank's operations. In other words, there is the suspicion that the bank processing the data for another bank will use the information to gain competitive advantages. In the main, this too is an unfounded concern, as most service providers have procedures to protect against the misuse of data and would not risk their computer operations to receive information by unethical methods, especially when most of such information can be obtained through other means.

In sum, the chief advantages of using another bank's EDP service would seem to be found in capitalizing on the experience and know-how already gained on common problems by the servicing bank and in minimizing one's start-up costs. In cases where a good correspondent relationship exists this advantage is further enhanced. The chief disadvantage would seem to be that few banks are really staffed to serve the individual needs of others. It is relatively easy for them to simply process another bank's items in the programs they have developed for themselves, but in point of fact, these programs seldom fit the specific needs of the bank desiring service. If the needed modifications are too costly, the result is usually a "forced fit" of the existing programs. It is advisable then for a bank seeking computer services to shop around and find another bank which can really meet its needs rather than vice versa.

2.1.2 Using a Service Bureau

This type of arrangement is similar in many respects to using a bank's service, and generally it will be helpful to use similar criteria to evaluate offers from service bureaus and banks. The service bureau has usually developed some competence in working with other banks and therefore has in stock a set of canned programs which it can apply. It may have the added advantage of having had extensive experience in general computer work outside the banking industry. Of course, the relevance of this outside work to banking problems will determine whether or not it enhances the overall service.

For evaluation purposes, service bureaus can be classified into two major groups. The first group includes those service bureaus which specialize in banking automation, and the second group includes those that provide computer services to several different types of industries of which banking is only one. Generally, the service provided by the service bureaus in the first group is more satisfactory for the bank shopping for off-premises arrangements. The major complaint against the service bureaus in the second group is that they often fail to appreciate the specific requirements of banks. Three specific complaints against this group often mentioned in the current study were:

*Lack of experience in setting up the initial system. In one bank this resulted in outright failure of the first conversion and brought its management close to a decision to drop the use of EDP altogether. While the service bureau managers were competent computer men, they had no experience in the special needs of banks and tried to apply systems used in other industries which were not appropriate for the bank.

*Lack of understanding of the importance of keeping to time schedules and deadlines in processing data. This happened when equipment broke down or other delays occurred in processing the work, and the banks found themselves without the needed information to proceed with regular day-to-day operations. The major problem was that the service centers lacked the flexibility or willingness to revise work schedules and priorities to accommodate the specific needs of the bank.

*The possibility that EDP services to other industries may become more profitable than service to banking to an extent that causes the latter to be ignored. In at least one case a midwest service bureau decided on relatively short notice to discontinue its services to banks and concentrate on other industries, leaving several banks in the area with a sudden need to find new service arrangements. In two other cases, bankers complained that the management of the service bureau was losing interest with regard to the development of further EDP applications for banking.

In the final analysis one will want to assess carefully the service bureau's capability and involvement in providing banking services. If it is a major part of the operation, then one could reasonably expect a more satisfactory experience than a situation in which there is little experience in banking services. It also stands to reason that service bureaus specializing in banking business will have more incentive to provide a good service since it is their primary source of income. In this respect, the service bureau might prove a better bargain than a bank which often gives priority to servicing its own work and meeting its own needs before those of banks using its services.

2.1.3 Participating in a Joint Venture

For several years the joint venture was held to be the ideal solution for the small bank which could not afford to buy or to lease its own computer but which desired to become deeply involved in automation. Evidence is accumulating, however, that joint ventures are not the panacea some envisioned them to be. Probably the most compelling piece of datum in support of this view is the relatively small number of banks which have chosen to go the route of the joint venture. The 1967 directory of bank joint-venture computer centers listed only 27 joint ventures where banks constitute the majority of the participants. These are owned by 212 participating banks.

There are some man-sized problems associated with joint ventures which we think account for their limited growth. Not the least of these problems is the very first task of arriving at an agreement as to the nature of the joint venture and the degree of participation of each of the banks involved. Even though the banks which enter into the joint venture are usually close geographically, they typically have very different individual circumstances in terms of the market they pursue and their goals. For example, one bank may wish to promote time deposits but may have little interest in consumer loans, while another bank might be promoting demand deposits and at the same time be heavily involved in consumer loans. In such a case where the resources which can be committed to a joint venture are usually quite limited, there must be compromises in terms of which applications are developed and in what order. These compromises are frequently difficult and painful to achieve.

A second outstanding difficulty has to do with the competitive position of the banks. The joint venture itself is based upon cooperation and the pooling of resources. At the same time, however, the banks which are cooperating are competing. It is extremely difficult for a member bank to overcome the feelings of proprietorship it naturally feels for a concept or a program which it develops. It is necessary then, to establish some guidelines in the very beginning of a joint venture which specify who will participate in what programs and who will foot the bill. The simplest agreement, of course, would be to have all programs available to all banks, but in cases where this agreement has been made, it is known that some banks have refused to develop programs which they desired because they were unwilling to have the other banks reap the advantages.

In any case, a bank's commitment to the whole process of automation is greater in a joint venture than in the other off-premises forms described. A center must be established, machines must be purchased or leased, people must be hired to design the programs and run the machines, and the entire venture must be managed. Herein lies a third major problem associated with a joint venture—management of the center. The number of persons with extensive knowledge of EDP who also have the management abilities to run a computing center is extremely limited. Moreover, it appears that managing a joint venture center requires a higher degree of management skill than managing a center for a single company. In the first place, the scope of the entire operation is considerably larger. Designing and implementing an application that will serve at the early stages as many as five to ten organizations requires a greater degree of flexibility and organization in all phases of the system. Yet, this is still basically a technical problem and can be handled by a competent EDP person. The real management problems lie in the areas of interacting with the management of the participating banks and balancing their individual goals and objectives.

A brief case history of a joint venture might be helpful to illustrate some of the above problems. One of the banks in the current study began a joint venture with nine other banks in 1960. The first activity of the joint venture was a feasibility study which culminated in proposals from several computer companies. In a short time they concluded they were not able to make an adequate evaluation of the computer proposals and subsequently hired a consulting firm to complete the feasibility study and make a recommendation to them. They then accepted the recommendation of the consulting firm and utilized members of both the consulting firm and the computer company chosen to develop their initial programs.

They decided to lease rather than to purchase equipment in order to minimize the initial investment. Each participating bank contributed $5,000 toward start-up costs. This amount enabled the venture to pay the consulting firm, get the equipment, and begin operations. Demand deposit accounting was the first program to be developed. When it was ready, the participating banks were converted one at a time. There was considerable variability in the smoothness with which banks were converted. The bank managers that we interviewed felt that this was a direct function of the planning and preparation which occurred in the bank. In their own case, the top level people became involved in the very beginning and carried it down to the lowest level in the bank. The result was a smooth conversion with no major problems.

This particular joint venture subsequently experienced three major problems, all of which could be traced to the initial organization. The center had been organized completely independently of all the banks involved. The manager of the center reported to a board of directors composed of one person from each of the participating banks. The other significant aspect of the organization of the center was an operations committee which was composed of the operations officer of each of the participating banks. This committee met approximately once a month and discussed future plans to recommend to the board of directors. It also served as a link between the computing center and the participating banks.

The first difficulty arose within the board of directors. The members found it virtually impossible to agree upon the orientation of the center or the emphasis which they would place on certain phases of the program. Yet, they feared that if they did not do something they would lose their competitive advantage to larger banks in the area that were already in the process of automating. A minimum degree of cooperation was finally "forced" on them because, as one manager put it, each was unable to pursue an automation program independently. In this particular instance, fear did not prove to be a very fruitful motivating force, as we will see below.

The second major problem which the joint venture faced was again a management problem but on a different level. The board agreed in principle that it should give the manager of the computing center a relatively free rein; yet in actuality it did not allow this. Over a six-year period it had three different managers of the center. The first manager was marketing-oriented and disagreed with the board about his role in the center. In essence, he wanted to move too fast for the board at this point. When the differences in outlook became too obvious he was replaced with a second manager. The second manager was hired because he appeared to be "more manageable" than the first. In the long run, however, it turned out that he did not have the ability to handle the job. He was eventually replaced with a third manager who is still on the scene but who has spent most of his time cleaning up the mess created by the first two. The board accepts the blame for much of this management fumbling. It feels that it has spent far too much time on operational problems of the center when it should have been focusing on broader problems such as long-range goals and objectives.

The third major problem faced by the joint venture was the participants' apparent inability to agree upon and develop new computer applications. After six years they had only demand deposit accounting, payrolls, and account reconciliation on the computer. This was not due to a shortage of personnel in the computing center. They had approximately 20 people operating the center, some of whom were qualified programmers. The development of new programs was inhibited instead by the competition between the banks. The joint venture was founded with an agreement that any program developed in the center would be available to all participating banks. The net effect of this agreement was to completely squelch any further developments than the programs initiated in the very first year.

Despite all these difficulties, the managers in the study felt they had profited from the experience. They indicated that they had entered the joint venture with one of their major goals being to learn about computer operations. The joint venture had made it possible for them to get a large number of people in the bank involved in the use of the computer. They attached a great deal of value to this educational process. In addition, they felt that the computer center had done a satisfactory job on the demand deposit accounting and that their savings in that area had been significant.

Although the bank was still participating in the joint venture at the time of our interviews, the managers had taken a hard look at their experience and were considering plans for their own computer within the next two years. They were firmly convinced that the glow had gone from joint ventures and that within ten years all joint ventures would disappear. In the words of one of the officers interviewed:

> "Joint ventures would be nice if bank managers thought alike; however, every bank is different. They have different markets, different organizations, different problems and different objectives."

Evidence suggests that the conclusion of this particular bank is probably accurate, albeit a little strong. Some joint ventures will continue to exist but because of competitive factors and different management orientations most banks will prefer to use a service or develop their own automation program.

2.1.4 Using a Holding Company
Computer Center

This arrangement may be regarded as a special form of the preceding two arrangements. In many cases, the bank which is closely held will not have the option of choosing the nature of its automation program. Typically, the decision to have a computing center which will service all companies owned by the holding company is made at a high level in the parent company without consulting individual member banks. Furthermore, once the decision is made, the individual banks have relatively little influence concerning the conversion of new applications, services and types of information to be furnished.

Probably the only significant difference between the holding company and the other off-premises arrangements has to do with the orientation of the computing center itself. Most holding company centers are responsible only to the parent company and have the general goal of balancing the service among all their member companies. Thus, a holding company center usually will not feel compelled to compete with the quality of service offered by another bank or service bureau. At the same time, the holding company has an interest to advance the banks under its control and usually does employ an expert computer staff, which the individual small bank could not afford.

2.1.5 Summary

The off-premises arrangements are especially suitable for the small banks with less than $50 million in deposits which cannot presently afford the level of investment required to develop an effective computer facility of their own. To be sure, many banks in this category can afford to acquire computing equipment, but having a computer on-premises and using it effectively are two very different things. There are some potential negatives in choosing an off-premises service. The bank that does so is giving up part of the freedom of running its own show and developing a dependency in the operations area on another bank or on a service arrangement. The bank may also lose out on some opportunities to expand its services to the customer, although this seems doubtful since more and more service providers are as eager to contract computerized customer services with banks as they are to sell data processing services for the bank itself. At the same time, the "off-premises" bank, if it takes advantage of the situation, can utilize the experience gained as a future springboard to its own on-premises computer operations.

There is need for caution, but not despair, on the part of the bank seeking an off-premises arrangement. In our opinion any size bank can participate in the modern revolution which EDP is causing in banking by choosing wisely among the alternative off-premises arrangements which are available. Any of them may be perfectly acceptable, but following are some of the questions which one should answer before making a decision.

*If a package program is being offered, does it really fit your situation and satisfy your needs? If not, is the service provider willing to make the necessary changes before conversion?

*What kind of assistance is the service provider prepared to offer in terms of orienting your own personnel and helping you through the initial conversion period?

*Is the service provider willing to take the necessary precautions in the transmission and handling of data in order to ensure its integrity?

*Does the service provider show evidence of flexibility and room for growth? That is, will he be able to develop more sophisticated programs as your needs change or is he already stretching his facility to serve you?

*Does the service provider have expertise and experience in servicing banks?

*Aside from the issue of capability, is there some reasonable evidence that the service provider values your business and will endeavor to improve his service to you as time passes?

*In case of an equipment breakdown, what kinds of back-up does the service provider have, and how will priorities on work to be processed be determined in such emergencies?

If the above questions relating to the quality of service provided are answered satisfactorily, and if the bank itself is prepared to make the necessary adjustments in its own system of operations, half the battle is won. In fact, however, very few banks follow through on a hard evaluation of their own needs or the services available. As a consequence they do not reap the maximum benefit from their data processing dollar, and many service providers continue to offer less than acceptable service and get by with it. In Chapters 3 and 4 we will discuss in more detail these problems and the means to handle them.

2.2 On-Premises EDP

Acquiring one's own computer involves the most complex set of decisions and the most extensive preparation of all the alternatives open to an organization. Management must consider the problems involved in setting up a new department, contracting for equipment and hiring or training people with skills not common to the banking industry. These exist for management in addition to the regular problems involved in choosing an off-premises arrangement. Moreover, whether the bank decides to lease or to purchase the equipment, the decision to use an on-premises computer demands a much greater commitment of resources in people and money.

2.2.1 Reasons for Choosing
On-Premises Computers

Many bankers who decide to acquire their own computers do so for a negative reason: namely, they do not trust off-premises services—especially if they are offered by another bank. In 12 of the 18 banks in the present study having on-premises EDP equipment, management stated that it did not seriously consider the possibility of using an outside service. (See Table 2.2.) Of those 12 banks, 9 explained that their main goal was to keep the bank independent, and therefore, they desired to keep "in-house" control of the operation. In the remaining three banks it was flatly stated that they did not trust the services offered by correspondent banks, mainly for fear of revealing competitive secrets. This belief existed in spite of the lack of any evidence of cases where it had occurred. On the contrary, it has been amply demonstrated that items can be sent out of the bank with adequate safeguards on privileged information and very little danger of losing the items themselves. At the same time, in seven of the banks the decision to get on-premises EDP was influenced by the feeling that it would serve the needs of the bank better.

Table 2.2

REASONS FOR CHOOSING AN ON-PREMISES ARRANGEMENT*

Reason	No. of banks
Keep the bank independent from others	9
EDP more flexible when under own control	7
Will be able to produce new revenues through customer services	5
Will be cheaper or of equal cost	4
Only arrangement available at the time	4
Do not trust the services of other banks	3
Feel experience to be essential for the future	2

*Most banks gave more than one reason for the decision.

Another reason for selecting an on-premises arrangement was the hope of offering automated customer services. Although only 5 of the 18 banks having on-premises EDP regarded this ability to offer customer services as a major reason for having on-premises EDP, 11 (61 per cent) of the 18 banks offered at least one service, and 9 (50 per cent) of them offered more than one type of service. At the same time, only 7 (23 per cent) of the 31 study banks using off-premises EDP offered any non-banking customer services, and only 2 (6 per cent) of them had more than one type of service.

On the whole, customer services do not appear to be particularly profitable for smaller banks at this time. A few of the study banks reported a great deal of enthusiasm for such services in the early stages of automation, but in fact, they had not developed them to the extent planned. One of the major reasons for the lack of development seems to be the small bank's unwillingness or inability to invest the necessary human and financial resources. Having a computer program, for example, to provide a payroll service is only part of the package; the bank must train personnel to administer the program as well as to promote and to sell it. Another reason is that computerized customer services require a relatively large initial investment which does not pay off for several years. A large bank can afford such an investment, and even when they are not directly profitable in the first few years, it may justify their existence as part of total banking service. For the small bank, however, this represents a diversion from the prime banking functions, a diversion it can ill afford.

Another frequent cause for choosing on-premises EDP is previous experience with tab equipment. Banks which had converted to tab equipment in the early 1960's are more likely to use on-premises computers of second or third generation than to switch to an off-premises service. In our study none of the banks initially using tab equipment switched to an off-premises service. In essence, tab equipment is an intermediate step between bookkeeping machines and computers such that the transition from tab to computer is a natural one and does not represent the kind of change involved in going from bookkeeping machines to computers. We are not recommending tab equipment as a first step towards automation for those banks facing the decision today; we are merely observing that historically, it has made the transition to computers easier. It is by no means a necessary step and in many cases would be an inefficient approach to automation.

2.2.2 The Need for Personnel

One of the major problems faced by bankers who decide to have on-premises EDP is the development of new skills and positions in the bank. Nine of the eighteen study banks reported greater staffing and interdepartmental problems than they had expected. Two main approaches can be taken to developing the skills of computer personnel. One is to train selected employees on the existing staff in the new EDP skills, and the other is to hire outsiders for the job. Of the 18 banks, half decided to use the first alternative and half, the second. (See Table 2.3.) Of the nine banks choosing outsiders for the supervision of EDP jobs, six reported considerable problems of adjusting the relationships between the newcomers and the regular staff. In four of those six banks, the problems finally resulted in the resignation of at least one officer in the bank. In part, the problems were caused by the almost inevitable resistance to change and the suspicion of new methods of work. Chapter 6 will deal in more detail with the attitudinal and perceptional problems related to the existence of EDP in the bank. Here, only the main factors felt at early stages of on-premises EDP installations are mentioned.

Table 2.3

STAFFING THE EDP DEPARTMENT

	Developed problems between EDP staff and other banking personnel		
Approach taken to staffing	*Yes*	*No*	*Total*
Trained own people	3	6	9
Hired outside people	6	3	9
Total	9	9	

Gaps in communication between EDP people and the remaining staff. Several EDP managers expressed frustration due to the feeling that the remaining managers did not understand what EDP was doing and should do. At the same time, banking officers complained that the EDP people did not understand enough about what they, the bankers, needed. In our opinion, both sides have a valid complaint. There is a very obvious communication problem, but both must share the responsibility for alleviating the problem. In order to work effectively together, both the EDP personnel and the traditional bankers must extend themselves especially at the early stages of an automation program to obtain at least a minimum understanding of the problems and the working tools of each other.

Salary differential and job mobility. Computer personnel are in great demand in all industries, and consequently, their salary level has been somewhat inflated in recent years. While larger banks can compete on this item, the average salary paid by other industries for comparable training and experience is almost always higher than that paid by small banks. In a few of our study banks, top management paid computer personnel at the same rate as other employees, and succeeded in holding them; in other cases, however, they had to pay them higher salaries, thus causing perceived inequities in the salary structure.

Difficulty in introducing innovation. While the initial conversion of the bookkeeping operation usually meets only mild opposition, the efforts to change basic procedures and to apply the computer in other areas often meets more resistance and consequently frustrates many EDP managers. Computer personnel are not noted for a great deal of human relations skill, so it is virtually inevitable that there will be opposition to the changes they introduce, and conflict will ensue. Much of this could be avoided by taking some minimum steps toward preparing the banking personnel in advance for the changes which will occur and including them, where feasible, in planning the changes.

An optimal approach to staffing an on-premise center, which would minimize conflict in the bank and still provide an effective automation program, is to combine "in-shop" and outside resources. The bank should try to identify an energetic officer in the bank who can best assume responsibility for running the center. He should be freed of all other tasks during the decision and conversion periods and should get outside training in all aspects of computers, including systems and programming. At the programming level, the center can be staffed by outsiders. Their main function will be technical in nature and they will be working under close supervision of the EDP manager. Thus it is not essential that they have traditional banking experience, although such experience is very useful.

2.2.3 The Equipment Factor

The bank interested in having on-premises EDP can choose between two major types of arrangements with the equipment supplier. It can lease the equipment or it can purchase it. Under the leasing arrangement, the bank usually pays a fixed rental per month which covers a certain number of hours of computer time. An additional charge is made for the time used above the minimum specified. Both types of arrangement should, and regularly do, contain a provision for servicing of the equipment by the manufacturer or the leasing company.

Sixteen of the eighteen banks utilizing on-premises EDP leased the equipment rather than purchased it. Only one of those regretted the decision after four years of using the same equipment. (It felt that for tax purposes, it would have benefited more by buying the equipment.) There are several good reasons why banks, like many other organizations, decide to lease rather than to buy the equipment.

Rapid changes in the equipment. Over the last decade, improvements in EDP have occurred at such a rapid pace that it would have been extremely costly to replace or update obsolete equipment that had been purchased. For example, some banks have changed their equipment four or five times over a period of ten years, moving from first generation to advanced third generation computers. Most banks recognize this and see that the only reasonably economical way for them to keep pace with technological advances is to lease equipment and change it when more suitable equipment is developed.

Changes in the use of EDP. The changing nature of banking, uncertainties concerning the introduction and spread of new services and development of existing applications, may result in a rapid obsolescence of the present computer system and a change in the user's computation volumes and tasks. Leasing is one means of minimizing these risks.

Encouragement by most manufacturers to lease rather than to sell the equipment. The ratio of buying price to monthly rental varies from 40/1 to 55/1, depending on the specific type of equipment. On the average, the manufacturer reaches a "breakeven" point in a leasing situation in four years; after that, the return from rentals will be mostly profits. Moreover, receiving the earnings in smaller amounts provides a considerable tax advantage to the manufacturer (Hamid, 1966).

The need to make a large one-time investment for purchase of a computer. Purchase prices can range from $250,000-$450,000 for small computers. Several bankers indicated they were afraid of their supervising agencies' reaction to such a large one-time investment.

In the computer industry as a whole there has been a decline in recent years in the percentage of computers rented and an increase in the percentage of purchases. The authors confess to having very little data on the economics of purchasing versus leasing EDP equipment; however, we do feel quite strongly that the decision cannot be based solely on economic analysis. (Other factors to be considered are discussed in Chapter 3.) The uncertainties in the introduction of new equipment, new developments in the banking industry, and the ultimate form which one's own use of the computer will take are such that the best economic analyses available may fall short.

Parallel to deciding whether to lease or to purchase the equipment, the bank has to select a specific manfacturer. The five leading computer manufacturers—International Business Machines (IBM), Burroughs, National Cash Register (NCR), General Electric (GE) and Radio Corporation of America (RCA)—supply over 98 per cent of the computers used in banking (See Table 2.4), with a sixth company, Honeywell, making strong efforts to penetrate this specialized market. Until recently, when the small bank considered computers, the choice was practically narrowed down to three manufacturers, IBM, Burroughs and NCR, because the other two offered

Table 2.4

COMPUTER CONFIGURATIONS USED BY BANKS

	Per cent of banks having on-premises EDP (619 surveyed)*
IBM	58.00
Burroughs	20.03
NCR	11.79
GE	7.27
RCA	1.13
Others	1.78

*All sizes.

SOURCE: ABA, 1968 Automation Survey.

mainly larger computers which the small bank either could not afford or did not need. IBM has a distinct sales lead and has for years supplied over half of all the computers to the banking industry. Being a leader in the market, the large manufacturer can frequently offer services that other manufacturers find hard to match, particularly in the areas of training facilities, maintenance service and back-up equipment. However, the number of services and their efficiency varies considerably from one region of the country to another, and a banker shopping for EDP is encouraged to examine the relative strengths of the manufacturers serving his area rather than to rely on national averages.

Each of the manufacturers usually has available several types of equipment which differ in capacity, ability to perform jobs, and cost (both initial investment and operating cost). The decision as to which type of equipment to select and why to select it is one of the key ones for the bank considering on-premises EDP. (This will be further discussed in Chapter 3.)

2.2.4 Summary

In almost every one of the study banks having its own computer on-premises there was evidence that the total operation involved a great deal more than had been bargained for. One consequence of this has been that many of the banks are unwilling or simply unable to invest the resources necessary to develop an effective program. The most obvious example of this can be seen in the area of investment in people. Many banks have refused to pay the going rate for qualified computer personnel and at the same time have not provided adequate training for their own people. The result has been a very low-level utilization of very expensive and potentially powerful equipment.

Having a computer service on-premises does permit a level of flexibility and potential for growth which might be hard to achieve using off-premises services. In the long run, it might also put the bank in a better competitive position than banks which did not elect to get their own computer. Nevertheless, for the smaller banks our guess is that if some of them had used the money and other resources spent on their own computing center to purchase computer service from an outside center and to give their own people some EDP training, they would be far ahead of the game.

Chapter 3

The Decision to Automate

The choice of the specific type of EDP arrangement is a complex decision which most bankers are ill-prepared to make. Aside from a careful economic analysis of the various forms available, there needs to be a thorough examination of the goals and objectives of the bank along with an exploration of possible strategies to achieve the goals. Part of this analysis, the whole of which is referred to as a feasibility study, involves technical issues with which bankers are usually unfamiliar. Another part deals with material which is familiar but in a different context. This chapter will attempt to clarify some of these issues.

The feasibility study is probably the most talked about, but least acted upon, phase in the decision to convert to EDP. In almost every study or textbook dealing with the introduction of EDP, a chapter or section is devoted to the need for and details of the feasibility study. (See: Dale, 1964; Judson, 1966; Rice, 1967; Sanders, 1966). Yet, of the 49 banks in our study that had made their decisions, only 12 conducted what could be considered a thorough feasibility study. (See Table 3.1.) Seventeen others conducted a partial study, and the remaining 20 did not carry out any study, examining only specific proposals which were advanced by possible service providers.

Table 3.1

THE USE OF FEASIBILITY STUDIES IN MAKING THE DECISION
TO AUTOMATE

Type of EDP decided upon	*On-premises EDP*	*Correspondent bank*	*Service bureau*	*Joint venture*	*Holding company*	*Total*
Thorough study conducted	6	1	1	4	0	12
Partial study of some aspect	7	6	2	0	2	17
No study—only proposal for services considered	5	5	4	1	5	20
Total	18	12	7	5	7	49

The broad aspects of a feasibility study can be summarized in the following steps:

1. Defining the goals and objectives of the bank and the system.
2. Taking inventory of the present system with regard to costs, personnel required, speed, accuracy and quantity of information generated and problems to be solved.
3. Designing a system that will achieve the objectives and resolve the problems facing the bank.
4. Soliciting proposals that will fit the planned system.
5. Evaluating the proposals and the impact of adapting them from an economic, technological and organizational point of view.

3.1 Defining Goals and Objectives

Lack of careful definition of the objectives and the problem facing an organization is seemingly too obvious a mistake to be made by anyone, but this is a common pitfall in introducing major change. Therefore, it is imperative that a bank examine where it wants to go in both the short- and the long-term before it makes such a significant decision as to which form of automation it will undertake. For many banks the kind of formal examination of goals and objectives to which we are referring will represent a new activity, but one which is likely to have significant payoff. The only three instances where this was even attempted in our study involved banks where the person responsible for the process was a junior officer who was required to report the developments in writing to senior management. However, in order for the decision to be effective, senior management itself should do the work. In the final analysis, the goals and objectives will depend to a large degree on past and present levels of activities, on the outlook for future growth and on market potential.

In addition to setting broad goals and objectives, the persons responsible for the automation need to make preliminary decisions on how they will approach the problem facing them. They can view it from one of several vantage points which are presented below in ascending order of their probable impact on the organization.

*Top management can view it as a decision regarding only a change of equipment. In other words, they can see themselves as simply replacing the present bookkeeping machines with different machines or eliminating them altogether by transferring the work to an off-premises service.
*They can view it as a decision affecting only the bookkeeping department. In this case, they would anticipate changes only within the bookkeeping department while other departments in the bank would continue to operate in the same fashion as before the conversion.
*They can view it as a decision involving only the internal information system and the operational procedures for existing services. In this instance the internal operational changes may be significant, but they do not come through to the customer.
*They can view it as a decision involving expansion of bank services and changes in management orientation. This, of course, involves radical change which is felt both internally and externally.

Beginning from one vantage point should not prevent the bank from considering the others at later stages of the decision, but an initial guideline through the expression of preference for one of the objectives is desirable. The last objective implies joining the industry's movement toward the retail-marketing orientation through the expansion of banking services. This is especially controversial for many banks. Some bank officers are excited about the potential and are urging their banks to proceed with dispatch to develop these services. Others are more skeptical about the return involved and still others consider these kinds of services to be inappropriate for banks. Our study would indicate that banks are certainly capable of offering such services and making a reasonable profit on them; however, this is a separate issue from the desirability of these services for the banking industry in general. It appears, in fact, that some of these issues will be settled in courts of law, as some banks have already been sued for what other business organizations consider inappropriate activity for banks.

The study also indicates that those banks which have decided to concentrate for the most part on traditional banking services find many applications for computers and still must choose from a wide variety of goals and objectives which may be pursued. In most of the study banks there was the immediate goal of relieving the heavy burden of clerical work in the bank. Goals such as improved information for management and improved controls on various banking functions have been secondary. However, a bank might well enter an automation program with the expectation that it will not save any money on personnel in the operations area (indeed, it might increase costs in this area) but that it will improve the information available to management for decision-making. This goal, if realized, could have a far greater payoff in the long run than savings in the clerical or operations area.

Under any circumstances it is important that management make a real effort to match its goals and objectives with its actual marketing environment. Each bank serves a unique market, and its information needs will vary as a function of the needs of this market. Two banks of equivalent size may be located in the same area and in one sense they compete, but in another sense, they may serve this market area in very different ways. For example, Bank A may concentrate on demand deposits and Bank B may concentrate on time deposits; or Bank A may specialize in real estate loans and Bank B may go after commercial loans. Even in a given functional area, the banks' goals, and therefore, their information needs, may be quite different. Thus, Bank A may have a large number of small individual accounts in the demand deposit area, whereas Bank B may focus strictly on industrial accounts without really caring about the number of individual accounts it has. Given this tremendous differentiation in the markets and goals, and therefore, in the information needs of banks, a single normative information system would have to include so many possible conditions that it would be impractical and useless. Therefore, it is essential not only to define the objectives of the bank as a whole but also the goals and strategies of each functional area which will contribute to the achievement of the organizational goals.

Normally, top management will set some guidelines regarding its preference of which functions to automate and in what order before the data collection for the feasibility study is started. These guidelines should remain flexible so that they can be altered as the feasibility study progresses. In most cases, the decision is a direct consequence of the operational pressures existing in the bank, which in turn are usually the key stimuli leading to consideration of EDP. In other words, the predominant strategy followed by virtually all of the study banks was to automate first the function that was giving them the most severe operational problems. This strategy provided the bank with the opportunity to realize substantial benefits from its automation program very quickly, but it also meant that the bank probably was choosing its most difficult application to undertake first. The goal of this approach is quite clearly one of relieving the pressure caused by the operational difficulties with only secondary attention being given to the most logical way to get into the process of automation.

Only one of the study banks had the latter consideration as its prime goal. Its strategy was to automate first a function which was running smoothly with no real problems under the manual system. It reasoned that it could achieve this easily and at the same time pick up valuable experience which would help in the conversion of each succeeding application. This approach seems to have a lot of merit. In the first place, it worked for the above bank, and secondly, the shock effect was less on the organization as a whole. Several banks that chose the most difficult application first had very demoralizing experiences which had some long-term negative effects on their total program. There is great value in having a successful experience on the first conversion beyond the mere cost of saving reprogramming time. A failure or a marginal success reinforces the pessimists in the organization and shakes the confidence of those who want to believe in automation but do not understand what is involved. A first application which is full of errors may cause some officers to distrust reports for months and even years to come.

3.2 Taking Inventory of Present and Future Operations

With the objectives defined and initial ground rules laid out, the bank should proceed to collect data on its existing system of operations and to make forecasts for the future wherever possible. The necessary information can be classified into several areas.

3.2.1 Present Level of Activity

Probably the most obvious factor which will determine which form of automation a bank will choose is the size of the bank. However, it is a little misleading to speak in terms of absolute size; what we are really referring to as the critical variable is level of activity. In general, the activity level increases as the size of the bank increases. However, there may be wide variations in activity level within a given size range of banks. For example, one bank with $20 million in deposits may be reasonably comfortable with a manual demand deposit accounting system to handle a relatively low level of activity, whereas another bank with the same amount of deposits but a much higher level of activity may find itself almost literally inundated with paper work. The data needed, therefore, are those regarding volume of activity in the various functions, the timing of peak and low periods, if they exist, the present process of operations and the key areas of difficulties.

3.2.2 The Information Network

The state of information technology makes it eminently feasible for a given bank to do a very thorough study of its information needs and', concomitantly, an evaluation of its information system. A series of questions must be answered in such a study. In brief, they are:

*What information is now available in the system for achieving the goals as defined?
*Is the information available being communicated effectively to all the relevant people?
*What additional information is needed in order to achieve the goals?
*What changes can be made in the information system to obtain the needed information and communicate it to the appropriate people?
*What information now present in the system is actually superfluous and therefore contributes to overloading the system?
*What steps can be taken to eliminate the superfluous information?
*What kinds of mechanisms can we build into the information system which will enable it to be self-correcting and self-improving?

The answers to these questions are likely to be quite revealing to an organization and may cause it to make significant changes in its strategies, organizational structure and system of operations.

3.2.3 Outlook for Future Growth

The data about the present level of activity and information network have to be related to the prospects for future growth.

One way of estimating potential growth is to look at the historical growth patterns of banks. This kind of data, however, can serve only as a general guideline when a bank is estimating its future potential. In the end, it must do a very careful analysis of its own immediate market situation and then relate its goals and objectives to this market. One reads in all the banking journals about how banks are becoming retail oriented and how they are expanding into various kinds of non-banking services. This is indeed true, and the computer is playing a significant role in the development of these services. However, it would be highly unrealistic for a bank to have as one of its major goals the development of some sophisticated non-banking services if it were not in a market area which would make use of such services.

3.2.4 Present Capabilities Relevant
to Automation

Taking its environment as given, the bank management must then assess its own capabilities and its internal potential for reaching its objectives. Some of the internal capabilities necessary to embark on an automation program are:

Physical space for computing equipment. Every bank which considers the alternative of having its own computer facility must take into account the space requirements of computing equipment. Many bankers are surprised to learn, however, that the actual physical space is only one aspect of this factor. What they learn sooner or later is that it must be a very special kind of space. Namely, it must be air conditioned; the floors must be capable of supporting a greater weight than is normally in an office; and it must have the capacity to carry much heavier loads of electrical current than the normal building is wired for. In short, to physically install and maintain a computing facility is no small task.

Substantial start-up costs for equipment and systems development. The costs involved in equipment and physical space are easy to compute and can be determined with a high degree of accuracy. For many small banks these costs will prove prohibitive and the bank will turn to some other form of automation on this basis alone. Other start-up costs are not so obvious and are much more difficult to estimate accurately. They include, in the first place, the cost of programming and systems development. One can make reasonable estimates of these costs, but it is best to expect that they will change and that it will require more time and more money than was first committed. These costs may be avoided, of course, with some forms of off-premises automation where the service already has existing programs which can be applied. In some other banks start-up costs exist, such as the need to number all the accounts and to encode checks, deposit slips and other items.

A bank which is about to undertake an automation program must be prepared to lay out a sizeable amount of cash from the very beginning of the program. In addition to the start-up cost, those responsible for the program should be assured of a fair amount of flexibility in their operating budget. They must be able to sustain their computer operation for some unknown period of time when costs will exceed income and/or savings.

Personnel. Launching an automation program will usually require some additional personnel or, at the very minimum, some training of present personnel. (The specific personnel problems and requirements are discussed in Chapter 7.)

There are several approaches to collecting the information in the above areas. Twenty of the study banks left the initiative of data collection concerning their own operations to outside salesmen who were interested in selling them the service or equipment. Whatever information was collected inside the bank was done only in response to a request by an outsider. As a result, in those 20 banks, either no records of the data collected were kept or they were in the form of some handwritten figures on scattered pieces of paper.

There are several explanations of why this occurred. Only one bank out of the 49 included in the study had an effective cost accounting system, and even there the system became effective only after the decision to install a computer was made. Because of the lack of cost data, it was difficult to establish the exact cost of segments of the pre-computer operation system and to determine exactly what changes would occur as a result of automation.

The bankers typically neglected the investigation of the information system with regard to reports, records and movement of information. The feeling of most of the persons responsible for collecting the information was that the bank was small enough for them to know all the details of the present information system without formally writing them down, and the end result was that very little attention was paid to the information aspects in the final evaluation.

The small bank especially has little recorded information about the market it is serving and its future prospectives. The senior officers know their particular customers well, but the bank as a whole lacks the ability to make forecasts about future growth. *The result is that the needs for automation are often based on present volumes and conditions rather than on those of the future.* Considering that in an on-premises installation the time difference between decision and actual conversion is often more than a year, this approach can lead to significant difficulties. In two of the banks where efforts were made to estimate future growth, the actual growth turned out to be twice as much as expected, and within six months of the installation there was a need for equipment with greater capacity.

It is highly recommended that the top management of the bank be involved in the data collection for the feasibility study and keep up with its development. This should not preclude the use of outside resources for advice and information source, but the major responsibility should remain within the bank itself.

3.3 Designing the System [1]

Due to the minimal amount of EDP knowledge in most small banks, the people involved in the decisions of whether and how to automate are not in a position to design the system most suitable for their bank. In only two of the banks was such an effort made. In the first, it was done by a computer expert who was brought into the bank to establish and manage the on-premises facility. In the other case, it was done by the manager of the joint venture with the help of a consulting firm, and a proposed system was outlined before proposals from manufacturers were solicited. In the remaining banks, the design of a specific system to fulfill the needs was left to the outsiders submitting the proposals for the service or equipment.

---

[1] For a more detailed discussion, see Moll, Robert E., "The design and implementation of a management information system," *Bank Administration,* October, 1968.

The end result is that the proposed systems are seldom detailed or comprehensive enough to actually serve the bank's needs in this area. About 80 per cent of the study banks "decided" by default to use the building-block or add-on approach in developing their automation programs. That is, they began with one application and then later added another without a clear strategy or long-term plan. They passed up the opportunity to design an integrated system which could be implemented in controlled phases.

If a thorough job has been done in defining objectives and taking stock of the bank's capabilities, then the system design will pose much less of a problem. While the bank may not have personnel who can specify the technical aspects of the system, they will certainly be able to work with outsiders in a more effective way so that the end product does match their expressed needs. The optimal system designed will be flexible enough to take advantage of changing situations and, at the same time, be outlined in enough detail to achieve the objectives and be helpful in the final decision of a specific manufacturer or service provider.

3.4 Soliciting Outside Proposals

Service providers and computer manufacturers are generally active in trying to solicit customers. Yet, by the time the bank comes to the stage of soliciting detailed proposals for final decisions, each bank has a limited number from which to choose. Thirty-five of the forty-nine study banks had only one complete proposal for consideration and another ten had two proposals from which to choose. In only one case, that of a joint venture, did the decision-makers have a total of four detailed proposals in front of them. In sum, although the average number of contacts with outside suppliers was 3.8 for each study bank, in the final analysis less than a third actually considered more than one proposal. This occurred for several reasons:

Premature decisions. In several cases an early decision had been made by the banks about the specific type of arrangement they were interested in. Once such a preference was indicated by senior management, serious proposals concerning other types of arrangements were discouraged.

Salesmen's time involved in preparing the proposal. The development of each proposal, especially for those interested in on-premises arrangements, takes considerable time and effort on the part of the salesmen. Because of the difficulty involved in getting cost and flow data concerning the conventional system, many salesmen are willing to spend the time involved only if they get some encouraging signs from management that their proposal has a reasonable chance of being accepted. This factor becomes less important if the bank is considering the use of correspondent bank service for which the proposal is usually much simpler and shorter.

Reluctance of bank officers to spend time supplying the needed data. Due to the lack of written records, most of the information collected by an outsider has to be done in face-to-face meetings with the operations people in the bank, who are often reluctant to spend any considerable amount of time dealing with several different salesmen.

Personal biases of the decision-makers. The officers involved in the decision process often have personal preferences for a specific proposal. In some cases, these biases are revealed only in the final stage of the decision (to be further discussed in section 3.6), but often the salesmen learn about them in an early stage of the proposal development and decide to drop out of the race.

3.5 Evaluation Phase

Most bankers are at a loss when faced with evaluating a computer proposal involving a good sprinkling of technical terms and a heavy dose of high-powered salesmanship. In cases where two companies were competing, the decision was often based on a better "impression" made by the salesmen of one of the two rather than on actual differences in the proposals. These "impressions" were also heavily influenced by the "expertise" gained in field trips.

Although proposals vary in specifics from one manufacturer to another, they all have similar established formats covering all or most of the sections described below. The proposal will usually be more detailed if submitted to a bank considering an on-premises arrangement and shorter to a bank considering off-premises arrangements. In some of the latter cases, the proposal might be merely a letter containing the prices for specific services with other details presented only orally.

A typical written proposal will contain the following parts.

System objectives and advantages. This will appear in some cases in the proposal itself and in other cases in an accompanying letter. It usually contains general advantages of an EDP system, with a flavor of a sales-pitch toward a specific proposal.

The proposed system. In the case of an on-premises proposal, it will contain the specifications of the equipment proposed, giving the names, numbers, and prices of the various parts of the system, but it will rarely contain an explanation of the operation of the equipment or detailed specifications. In the case of an off-premises proposal, this section usually will be omitted.

Specific applications. In the majority of proposals, only the applications considered for immediate conversion will be outlined. This leaves the decision-maker at a disadvantage when he wants to consider long-term applications. Only in a few proposals, notably those of IBM, were most or many possible applications discussed.

Installment needs and cost. The cost is usually broken down into the initial cost of starting the operation and into operating costs. In most cases, however, only the direct costs are included; indirect costs incurred through the involvement of non-computer bank personnel in the process of conversion are not mentioned.

Personnel needs and savings. Again, in most cases, only direct additions or deletions to the operations staff are discussed. Several bankers complained that although they saved personnel in the data processing sections, new personnel had to be added in other functions, bringing the total saving to much below the expected levels or in some cases, erasing it altogether.

Operation time. The times given for processing data are usually the *optimal* times required by the central processor and do not provide realistic estimates of time involved in the total operation. The result is often considerably less saving of actual operation time after the conversion than what was promised in the proposal.

Training needed for the bank employees. In many proposals, this section is missing altogether. In others, it contains a listing of what is available rather than of the specific needs of the bank considered.

Assistance by the supplier. In recent years, proposals have tended to place more emphasis on this section, outlining assistance in installment of the system, conversion and maintenance. The weakness of the section usually lies in its generosity in specifying what is available, rather than in defining a specific program of assistance.

Time table. In most cases this does not appear in the proposal and is left to negotiation or, in a few cases, to letters of intent after the decision has been made.

Types of reports. Although the output reports are going to have a major impact on the bank, only in a few cases are they outlined in detail in the proposal.

A general impression obtained from reviewing proposals when they were available, was that they were directed toward the average bank, rather than outlining a system and program for the specific bank receiving the proposal.

Visits to existing installations are very popular and are usually made by all the people involved in the decision process. A few years ago the trend was to invite the bank representatives to visit an exhibition center located in the plant or sales office of the equipment manufacturer. But the bankers often resented the idea of being shown a "mock-up" demonstration and preferred to see the equipment in operational conditions. Therefore, almost all visits today for bankers interested in an on-premises arrangement are made to installations operated by other banks. In the case where an off-premises service is considered, visits to the correspondent bank or service bureau are arranged.

Such visits were arranged in all the study banks; in many cases, the entire senior management, even those not directly involved, took part in them. The usefulness of such visits for anything but impressing the visitors is doubtful. In a short visit, lasting only a few hours, the person without previous EDP knowledge has little chance of understanding what is happening and of learning about operational procedures and problems involved. In eight of the participating study banks, members of the boards of directors were also invited to visit EDP installations and made their decision to approve the automation plan based primarily on their short visit.

More useful than the short visits to installations are the training sessions sponsored by the computer manufacturers to which bank representatives are invited even before the bank makes its decision. The programs range from three days to two weeks and are offered mainly to the operations officers in the bank. The person guiding the decision process will, in most cases, be invited to at least one such program if the salesmen feel there is a possibility that the bank will use an on-premises arrangement. In such programs the participants learn about equipment capabilities, problems of conversion, and development of programs. In several of the study banks the information the bankers accumulated during the program was essentially all that they knew about EDP, and thus it influenced their final decision considerably.

3.6 The Moment of Truth

By the time a bank has arrived at the final decision phase, it usually has already developed preferences for one type of arrangement or another. Below are summarized some of the reasons given for choosing the specific equipment or the specific service.

3.6.1 On-Premises Arrangements

The reasons for the final choice varied among the banks, but it is important to note that the cost factor was not the only one considered or even the most important one. In addition to comparing the specific cost arrangements, the following factors were involved:

Experience with the bookkeeping equipment the bank used before the arrival of the computer. Seven of the banks chose the equipment of the same manufacturer that supplied them their bookkeeping equipment in the past because they were satisfied with the service they received. An eighth bank refused to consider a specific manufacturer because it felt the experience with the old bookkeeping equipment was disappointing.

Relative strength of the specific manufacturer in the area. Due to the lack of technical knowledge of the equipment, many small banks have to make the choice with insufficient data. Here, the influence of uncertainty avoidance was strongly felt. The decision-maker will be inclined to choose a manufacturer of a machine that has already been used in the area, preferably by another bank, and about which no complaints were heard. Four of the banks mentioned this as one of the reasons for their final choice.

Previous acquaintance with the specific equipment. If the person guiding the process or one of the main supporters had been exposed to the equipment and had favorable impressions, he would push for choosing this type of computer. In one bank, one officer involved in the decision described it as follows:

"We chose XYZ after our operations officer returned from a two-week course to which he was invited by XYZ. He came back so impressed that we had no choice."

A similar explanation was given by two other people interviewed in the same bank. In two other banks, a specific computer was chosen because one of the people involved in the final decision had been exposed to the same type of equipment in other banks.

Promises of help in installation, programming, and service. The written proposals of the various manufacturers are usually quite similar in the description of the services offered to the bank using their equipment. The difference often lies in the oral promises made by the salesmen. All will usually add additional promises to help, especially during the conversion time, which were not specified in the written proposal or contract. Here, the decision-maker's personal trust in the sales representative, and the image the salesman makes during his contacts with people in the bank, can make a difference in the final choice.

3.6.2 Off-Premises Arrangements

The choice here is simpler than the previous one. The bank looking for an off-premises arrangement already has at this stage a strong bias toward choosing a specific proposal. The main factors influencing the decisions are:

Previous acquaintance with the service provider. Two of the study banks which chose a correspondent bank indicated that, from the beginning, only one offer was seriously considered, although in one case more were submitted. In both cases, the service provider was a large correspondent bank which had helped the study banks on various occasions in other matters and therefore had an inside track in the competition to offer computer services.

Pre-determined bias against some proposals. It was mentioned earlier that many bankers fear that their competition will have an advantage if the latter processes their work. Therefore, proposals submitted by banks in the same competitive area are frequently eliminated in the final stage of decision-making.

The reputation the service providers have established for themselves. If the service bureau or the bank is already providing satisfactory services to other banks in the area, they will have a distinct advantage over a new service bureau or bank just starting to sell such services.

Cost of service. While equipment manufacturers seldom offer discounts, the off-premises service provider will often do so to meet a competitor's offer. Therefore, there will be little price differential among the various offers, and price will not be a major factor in the final phases of the decision.

Other factors, such as the type of reports to be supplied and assistance in the conversion, are sometimes discussed at earlier stages but usually play only a secondary role in the final decision, despite their critical importance.

3.6.3 Joint Venture Arrangement

A bank evaluating the decision to join a cooperative effort faces two different decisions at this stage. The first and most important is the decision of whether or not to join the other banks and participate in the venture. A positive answer may mean a sizeable commitment of capital as well as an adjustment of management philosophy. Specifically, confidence in the ability of the several banks to come to compromise decisions must be substituted for freedom of independent action. In three joint ventures participating in this study, there were banks that decided at this stage not to join because they did not feel ready to commit themselves to the special requirements of a joint venture. This left the remaining banks with a decision of whether to continue at an additional cost without the dissenters or to drop the idea altogether. In all cases, at this stage the participating banks found themselves so committed to the idea of using EDP through a joint venture that they decided to stay in.

The second decision is the choice of the specific equipment. This is handled in a similar way to that of banks deciding on on-premises arrangements.

3.7 Summary

As indicated above, the execution of a feasibility study is one of the weakest points in the small bank's decision to automate. This is true despite evidence that this phase in the decision-making process is critical for the long-term success of an automation program. The banker making the decision needs guidance in conducting such a study, but frequently he does not take advantage of available sources of help. It is probably more effective if the bank can conduct its own study, but as an alternative or supplement, the bank can request the help of independent consultants who will conduct or supervise the feasibility study and present the data to the bank's management for a final decision.

In making the choice of a specific proposal it should be remembered that the decision to accept one proposal over another depends on more than just cost comparisons. Also to be considered are previous experience with manufacturers' equipment or the service provider, reputation of the center, the availability of service, assistance with conversion and back-up equipment, the type of reports and other services supplied, and future expansion potential. This part of the decision process should be the responsibility of top management, with the assurance that the other people involved understand the information presented to them and the consequences of choosing one proposal over the other.

We have touched on costs in a variety of contexts in the above discussion, but we have not focused on comparative costs *per se* of various alternative forms of automation. Ideally, a bank should perform a thorough cost-benefit analysis before making its decision. In most cases, however, there is only a rather informal comparison of the costs and potential savings involved in several alternatives.

A comprehensive cost-benefit analysis requires an integration of all of the factors discussed in this chapter. Few banks are prepared to spend the time and the money required to complete such a study. Consequently, some banks embark upon automation programs which are far too ambiguous for their needs, while others begin programs which are far too inadequate for their present as well as future requirements. We think all would be better off to spend the necessary time and money in the study phase to introduce as much rationality as possible into this complex decision-making process.

Chapter 4

The Conversion Period

Following the decision to launch an automation program and the selection of a specific proposal, the bank must proceed to plan and execute the conversion to EDP. In actuality these are not discrete steps but rather an integral part of the entire decision-making process described in the previous chapter.

Of the 57 banks included in our study, a great majority encountered some difficulty in automating their operations. The cause could usually be traced to inadequate preparation in terms of planning, training personnel, dealing with possible employee resistance, and modifying the existing procedures. In short, there was a reluctance to commit the human and financial resources required to cope with the changes being undertaken. A fairly common attitude on the part of senior bank officers was that once the decision to automate had been made, the actual conversion would be a routine, largely mechanical, operational problem which could be handled by lower echelon officers. On the contrary, it is only through the continued active involvement of top management and operations officers in the planning and execution phases that a smooth conversion can be assured. Following are some of the more critical issues.

Planning and time commitment on the parts of management and other employees. Regardless of the form of automation chosen, this increases considerably, at least in the short run, as compared to the time resources invested in making the decision.

Training needs related to the change to EDP. These include immediate training of those directly responsible for operating the new system as well as orientation of others in the bank whose jobs will eventually be affected by the conversion.

Organizational changes required by the conversion. The pre-EDP operational system has to be re-examined and the necessary changes carefully planned to provide for an effective conversion.

Possible resistance to change. This might arise from three different groups: management not directly involved in the decision process, non-management employees and customers.

System reliability. Since the computer is capable of handling significant amounts of data and information processing, it is possible to make "larger-than-life-sized" errors if appropriate safeguards are not built into the system. Two areas of importance here are program debugging procedures and integrity of input.

4.1 Planning and Commitment of Resources

A major cause of difficulty in converting to EDP is inadequate planning. To be sure, it is difficult to arrive at accurate estimates of financial and human resources required to automate. In preparing such estimates, bankers, like many other managers, try to minimize the budget allocated to accomplish the job. What they often do not consider, however, is that while top-notch computer men are expensive in terms of average salary scales in banking, their presence can lead to significant long-run cost savings by means of more efficient and widespread use of the EDP equipment and the information generated by it. The same may be said for users of off-premises equipment; i.e., having a liaison man who understands both banking and computers can be much more effective than having a banker without computer knowledge serving in this capacity. It is probably irrelevant whether this liaison is a banker or computer expert initially, so long as he is adequately trained in the other field before he assumes the responsibility.

Equally as important as the commitment of financial and human resources is a realistic time commitment. By this we mean that adequate time should be allowed for planning and designing the system, training other employees (or providing for their training) and implementing the conversion. Often this calls for restraint on the part of the original decision-makers, who are naturally anxious to see relief from the crisis which precipitated the decision in the first place.

The length of time between the decision to use EDP and the first successful run on the computer depends on several factors:

1. The type of arrangement chosen by the bank.
2. The approach taken in the development of the automation program.
3. The urgency felt among the decision-makers in banks as to when computer services are needed.
4. The amount of resources in money and people invested in the conversion process.

The average length of time between the decision and first successful application was 8.7 months for the study banks. It was much lower for those using off-premises EDP; there the average was 4 months and the range 1.5-6.0 months. It should be noted that the one bank that converted within a month and a half after making the decision to automate ran into considerable problems and had to convert the same function twice. The remaining banks had only minor problems during the conversion which were not attributed to the time element.

By comparison, it took the banks using an on-premises arrangement an average of 13.2 months to achieve the first successful run. The longer time was due in part to the time required for obtaining the equipment from the manufacturer, for the average length of time between the arrival of the equipment and the first run was close to three months. However, the banks were actively preparing for the conversion while waiting for the equipment to be delivered so it is difficult to assess how much of the total time could have been reduced had the delivery time not been a factor.

During the period between the decision and the conversion at least one person in each of the study banks spent all his time on conversion planning and preparation. In most of the banks additional people were involved full or part-time. In the banks having their own computers, an average team of three people was involved in preparation for conversion, while in the banks using off-premises arrangements, the average was 1.5 persons.

This demand on the time of the employees caused complaints from top management and the operations people in several banks. The preparation for EDP had to be assumed in addition to the bank's daily data processing work. The inability to postpone operations for longer periods of time and the removal of key operations people from the day-to-day work brought pressure on other employees and management. In most cases, top management had not expected the conversion to consume so much of the key people's time. It is difficult, if not impossible, to make a normative statement regarding how much time should be taken in the conversion process.[1] It will depend in large part on the bank's approach to the whole process of automation.

There are two distinct ways to develop automatic data processing systems. Most organizations choose the adding-on or building-block approach as they find it the least disruptive to the ongoing organizing activity. To be specific, most of the study banks chose one function at a time and automated that function basically, as it was currently being performed manually, without considering the interrelationships between that and other functions and the changes which might have been indicated as a result of these interrelationships.

The systems approach, on the other hand, looks at total purpose and usually leads to a fresh, functionally designed system. It avoids the larger error of getting "locked into" certain procedures or reports, which often happens when one builds on existing systems as described above. Methods changes in certain operations may take on less importance if one works backwards from a goal. Instead of saying, "This is what we're doing, let's automate it," the systems approach asks, "What do we want? How do we get it? Which part of the operation should be automated?" This approach will usually require considerably more time and human resources in preparation for the conversion than the building-block approach. In ideal terms it is by far the more desirable of the two approaches, but to many executives it appears too time consuming. It is probable, however, that the long-term efficiencies realized would far outweigh the initial time required for start-up.

4.2 Training for Conversion

There are certain training issues which are common to all banks deciding to automate. They can be divided into two separate areas. The first is orientation training, i.e., imparting general knowledge of what the computer is doing and what it can do for the bank. The second is training in those aspects of the person's job which will be immediately affected by the conversion.

None of the 57 banks studied conducted any sort of integrated, formal training program before converting to EDP, and we believe this to be a major cause of difficulties encountered in the conversion. The closest thing to an orientation program for tellers and supervisors in the study banks was an explanation of new output forms and specific instructions about input

---

[1]In a sense the conversion process is a continuous one as a given organization will never stop adding new functions or changing existing ones. Practically speaking, however, the conversion period refers here to the time required to get the first significant applications operational.

preparation to those directly affected. This is necessary but not sufficient. At best, employees were made familiar only with the particular operation for which they were responsible. They should have also been made aware of the significance of computers in general and of the implications of the bank's specific automation program for their particular function and the bank as a whole.

Of the questionnaire respondents, 46 per cent indicated that there were at least some problems as a result of insufficient training in new procedures and 15 per cent indicated there were serious problems. The situation was somewhat worse in those banks using off-premises services, where 18 per cent of the respondents indicated serious problems, compared to only 11 per cent in the banks using on-premises EDP. (See Figure 4.1.) As one might expect, size of the bank is a critical factor in this area; the larger the bank, the greater the need for training or the more likely problems will emerge in the absence of training. This was confirmed in the current study where 65 per cent of the respondents in banks with over $25 million in deposits indicated the existence of problems attributable to lack of training as compared to 56 per cent in those under $25 million.

Managers who were not directly involved in the EDP decision process usually received even less training or education about the role of the computer than did clerical employees. "Training" usually consisted of showing them where certain pieces of information were to be found in the computer-generated reports. Moreover, in some instances the construction and the distribution of reports was determined on the basis of individual judgments by the EDP personnel, with little regard for either the kinds of information actually needed by various managers or the forms in which they would like it presented. In other cases, the EDP manager did conscientiously consult each officer to try to ascertain his needs, but managers usually were unable to respond effectively. Part of the reason for this is lack of understanding of the computer system and therefore, inability to know what is possible. Also, because the EDP decision was primarily motivated by severe operating pressures, inadequate attention was devoted to the training necessary for optimal use of information.

When asked what types of training they would like most for themselves, the majority of officers in our study banks mentioned reading and interpreting output and learning about the capabilities of the computer. This training should be an integral part of a program in preparation for conversion, rather than an afterthought. As it is now, many of the reports that are produced often go unread, due to the tendency to print in report form practically all the information in the computer's memory. This intensifies the very "paper explosion" computers were intended to avoid.

In sum, the present practice of giving only on-the-job technical training will not suffice in the future. Employees at all levels should be given more comprehensive education as part of the basic indoctrination program. The specific content of parts of the program may differ for various levels and functions in the bank, but all employees should have a good idea of how EDP will operate in the bank and the ways it will affect methods and procedures in various parts of the system. This may well call for sending employees to relevant seminars and courses away from the bank or assigning blocks of time for training on-premises. Many bankers felt they could not afford to "lose" people for large blocks of time as would be required for such training, but we feel they cannot afford to do otherwise.

FIGURE 4.1 EXTENT TO WHICH INSUFFICIENT TRAINING IN THE NEW PROCEDURES CAUSED PROBLEMS IN AUTOMATING INFORMATION PROCESSING IN THE RESPONDENT'S BANK

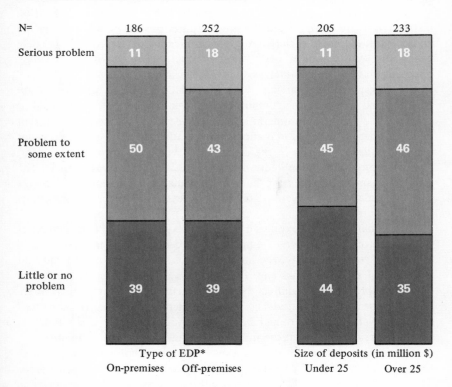

*Statistically significant difference at α= .01 level.

4.3 Modifying the Organization

For the most part, conversion to EDP has had little effect on the organizational structure of the bank, except for the rearrangement of the data processing system. Here, the major change has occurred in the bookkeeping department. Some of the clerical workers in the old bookkeeping department were transferred to new jobs in EDP-related areas, such as keypunching Others remained in their old jobs such as answering tellers' and customers' inquiries and were retrained in locating the necessary information on the new report forms. The problems this caused were relatively minor, usually involving individual workers more than the organization as a whole. Thus, at the time of conversion, structural changes were kept to a minimum. There is, however, an apparent increase in the number of problems resulting from modifications of the organizational structure with an increase in size of the bank's deposits. While only 31 per cent of respondents in the under $25 million group indicated such problems, this percentage rose to 40 in the above $25 million group. Another factor in determining the degree of changes in structures is the number of branches and the pre-computer operation methods in these banks. When the pre-computer processing was done at the branch level, automation caused a more significant shift of workers. In some banks this was combined with the introduction of the new marketing orientation at the branch level, as discussed in Chapter 1.

One organizational variable to be considered during the conversion planning and in which the computer has played a major role in the bank is control. As a result of automation, top management is able to obtain current information on operations so that preventive, rather than corrective, decisions may be made. Yet many of the control devices are discovered by accident, and many more are undoubtedly directly available if a request is made. The problem again is to encourage busy bank managers to sit down and decide what information they would like and how existing information might be used for control purposes.

Several bank officers expressed the initial expectation that the computer would reduce the number of employees needed and that this would help offset EDP costs. In reality, the number of jobs has either remained constant or increased slightly. Banks have found, however, that this same number of employees processes a significantly greater quantity of items, which essentially represents a unit cost saving. The slight increase in managerial personnel is caused by the addition of an EDP department or computer liaison function and the increasingly evident expansion in customer services now possible.

To sum up, while major organizational changes are not a necessary part of the initial planning for EDP, attention should be devoted to long-run effects. The minimal impact of EDP on organizational structure and procedures to date can be attributed to a number of factors, including inexperience with the new systems, lack of understanding of how to utilize them more effectively, and natural and predictable resistance to change in existing structures and procedures. In the long run, those bankers who plan for changes in structure and procedures to take advantage of the potential of the new systems and equipment should command a significant business lead over the bankers failing to do so.

4.4 Resistance to Change

It is almost inevitable that an organization will experience some employee resistance with the introduction of a change as significant as EDP. In the study banks most of the resistance came from clerical employees and officers who were not involved in the decision process to introduce EDP. Also, more resistance was found in banks with on-premises facilities than in those using an off-premises service. This fits the general picture of an on-premises facility having a much greater general impact on the bank than an off-premises service.

As one might expect, the EDP officers felt employee resistance to a greater extent than other managers. In this group, 57 per cent indicated resistance was a problem to some extent, or a serious one, compared to only 35 per cent of the total sample who felt this way. These officers are, of course, the first to feel the impact of such resistance, but the results might also indicate that the resistance was mainly at the operational level and therefore not recognized by the top executive officers, of whom only 34 per cent said it was a problem. Figure 4.2 reveals that among the younger officers, a large group (48 per cent) felt that employee resistance caused some serious problems, and the percentage of officers feeling this way declined with increase in age, to a low of 19 per cent in the oldest age group. This again supports the notion that resistance is confined mainly to the lower operational level, where the younger officers have to deal with it.

Three major factors seem to account for the resistance. The first, and perhaps the primary cause, is lack of information about the conversion among employees not involved in the decision process. Fear of being immediately replaced by the computer was not the problem, as all of the study banks assured their employees that they would be retrained either in the new procedures of their present function or in a new position. Rather, the problem was the fact that only limited information was supplied to employees once the decision to automate had been made. Thus, rarely was an individual made fully aware of how his particular function fit into the total system. It seems clear to us that employees were resisting these "unknown" changes much more than the known ones.

FIGURE 4.2 EXTENT TO WHICH EMPLOYEE RESISTANCE WAS A
PROBLEM IN AUTOMATING THE INFORMATION PROCESSING IN THE
RESPONDENT'S BANK (CLASSIFIED BY AGE GROUP).

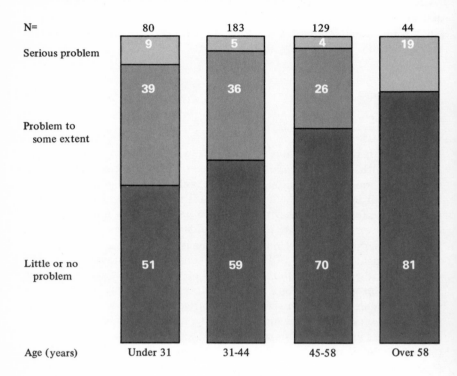

One vice-president in charge of operations put it this way:

> "Before computers, you could teach by demonstration and you
> could show a cause and effect relationship between what an individual
> is doing and what the results were. In many instances now, however,
> people are simply working with results, and they are not sure how the
> results were arrived at. This often leads to a mistrust of information."

A second cause of employee resistance was the necessity to give up the
"tried and true" ways of doing things under new operational methods and
techniques. Complaints were common among long-time employees, particularly bookkeepers whose jobs would be most affected by EDP, simply
because they were used to the present system. An example of a procedural
change which led to much resistance in the study banks was the change from
posting customer information on ledger sheets to posting it in a daily journal
of all customers' transactions. This means that to reconstruct a particular

customer's activities, the employee must go back to previous daily journals rather than consult just that customer's ledger sheet. Unless the reasons for such a change are outlined for the employee, it is not difficult to understand his discontent.

A third reason for employee resistance is fear of loss of authority, power or prestige. The EDP officer, who is often a new employee and a young one at that, may by-pass the head of bookkeeping or other key operations persons in planning the conversion, dealing instead with a top-level manager. The practice may indeed lead to greater efficiencies in designing the system, yet in at least five of the banks studied the discontent it caused raises some doubts as to the ultimate value of by-passing such key personnel.

Employee resistance may manifest itself in several ways. One of the most common, though not necessarily intentional, is insufficient attention devoted to the preparation of information to be used as input for the computer. This can result in costly errors and delays. While inadequate training is undoubtedly a factor, many officers interviewed attributed it to resistance as well. Another form of resistance is the internal communication of complaints, where the computer is blamed for mistakes or failure to perform as anticipated. This leads to a general reduction of motivation, as a scapegoat has been found to accept the burden for employee inadequacies. Finally, employees may simply ignore computer output. This form of resistance is more subtle and passive but can be just as harmful to the organization as the first two. Those engaging in this kind of resistance profess to prefer the old sources of information and consult computer output only when forced by circumstances.

The use of EDP has had two major effects on customers. The first was the use of numbers rather than names to identify accounts. The second was the introduction of encoded checks and deposit slips which could be used only for the specific account bearing the encoded number. In the early days of automation, many customers were dissatisfied with these two innovations, especially the second one. Together with early programming problems in some banks, the two changes caused an undetermined number of customers to move from automated banks to non-automated ones.

In the last couple of years, this form of customer resistance has almost disappeared. Bankers still mention cases of a few stubborn customers who refuse to use encoded checks or deposit slips, but it has ceased to be a serious concern. Only in one bank did customer resistance become a serious problem when the bank changed from a detailed monthly statement to a "Bob-Tail" one.[2] The bank was located in a small town where the two other banks kept

---

[2] "Bob-Tail" statements list only the beginning and end balances, number of transactions and in some cases the sum of deposits and withdrawals during the month. The full statement will list each transaction with date and other reference information.

using a full statement, and because of customer objections and transfer of accounts to rival banks, the bank had to return to the use of the full statement.

In sum, minimizing employee resistance requires sufficient training and preparations for EDP, involvement of the relevant people in the planning and decision-making processes, and an effective communication system to inform employees about the changes and their implications. Anticipating possible forms of resistance to automation can contribute significantly to a smooth conversion. The prevention of such resistance should be an integral part of the EDP planning process, of concern to top management as well as EDP and operations officers.

4.5 Systems Reliability

In several of our study banks significant problems developed during conversion which could be traced to inadequate debugging or poor preparation of input. As one is nearing completion of a program there is frequently a great felt urgency or desire to get it operational as fast as possible. Trouble almost always follows if this desire forces out careful procedures.

Programs that are put to use before being completely "de-bugged" result in errors in the output, which in turn cause considerable frustration to the employees. The highest level of frustration was expressed in those banks using an off-premises arrangement, excluding those using a correspondent bank computer. That is, in banks using a holding company, joint venture or service bureau computer, 53 per cent of the respondents expressed such frustration, compared to only 32 per cent in banks using on-premises EDP and only 29 per cent in those using a correspondent service. (See Figure 4.3.)

The high percentage can be explained by the lack of experience of many computer centers under those three arrangements. This is compounded by the distance of the computer center from the bank, which prevents early interception and correction of mistakes. While new on-premises establishments often suffer from the same experience, their being physically close to the operation helps them respond more quickly and in person to errors, thereby reducing the frustration. The main reason why frustration is lowest among users of correspondent banks is that most of the banks providing such services do it only after the system has been pretty thoroughly debugged.

The people who complained most about errors caused by the program are the bookkeeping employees, where 68 per cent complained about the frustration caused (Figure 4.3). They act as intermediaries between the data processing section and the other employees, or even the customers, and usually are the first to discover the errors. Another group frustrated by such errors is that

FIGURE 4.3 PERCENT OF RESPONDENTS AGREEING WITH THE
STATEMENT: IN OUR BANK WE HAVE EXPERIENCED CONSIDERABLE
FRUSTRATION BECAUSE COMPUTER PROGRAMS WERE PUT INTO
EFFECT BEFORE THEY HAD BEEN THOROUGHLY "DE-BUGGED" AND
CORRECTED.

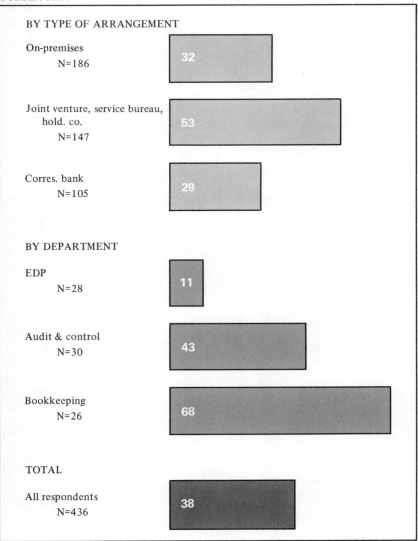

BY TYPE OF ARRANGEMENT

On-premises
    N=186   32

Joint venture, service bureau,
    hold. co.
    N=147   53

Corres. bank
    N=105   29

BY DEPARTMENT

EDP
    N=28   11

Audit & control
    N=30   43

Bookkeeping
    N=26   68

TOTAL

All respondents
    N=436   38

of audit and control (43 per cent), as they find difficulties in fulfilling their task
if such errors exist. At the same time, very few computer people (11 per cent)

admit to the use of programs which have not been debugged; they prefer to see the reasons as errors in input preparation.

Errors resulting from incorrect preparation of input were more prevalent in banks using on-premises EDP, where 57 per cent of the respondents saw it as a problem, compared to only 42 per cent of those using off-premises EDP. (See Figure 4.4.) This is mainly a result of the lack of experience in the new EDP operation and insufficient training. While most off-premises service providers had some previous experience in preparing input for the computer and could teach it to the bank employees, such knowledge is usually lacking at a new on-premises installation.

FIGURE 4.4 EXTENT TO WHICH ERRORS IN PREPARATION OF MATERIAL FOR THE COMPUTER WERE SEEN AS A PROBLEM IN AUTOMATING THE INFORMATION PROCESSING IN THE RESPONDENT'S BANK

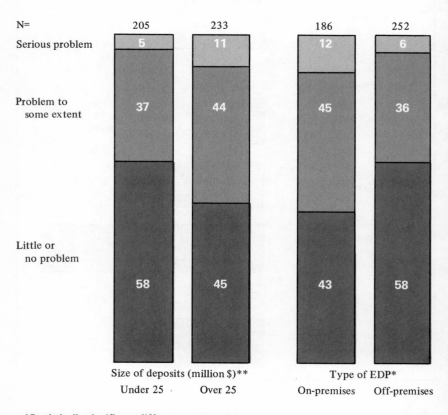

*Statistically significant difference at =.01 level.
**Statistically significant difference at =.05 level.

The problem was also more evident in the larger banks (over $25 million in deposits), where 55 per cent complained about such problems, compared to 42 per cent in the smaller banks. In the larger banks, it is often more difficult to locate the source of error and prevent future errors than it is in the smaller bank with a small staff and less activity.

4.6 Some Practical Decisions Regarding Conversion

In Section 4.1 two general approaches to conversion—the systems and the building-block approach—were discussed. Keeping in mind the critical issues discussed above, some practical decisions which are relevant to both should be reviewed. Several of these decisions are common to all banks, regardless of the type of arrangement used, while others are directly related to the specific arrangement chosen.

Those decisions common to all banks include the following questions:

*Should an exact timetable and step-by-step conversion plan be outlined or should the problems be approached one at a time, moving to a next step only if the previous one is satisfactorily solved, with no time constraint?
*Should the conversion of a given application be done in divisable sections or should the whole function be converted at once?
*Should there be a parallel run of the old system until the new system runs smoothly or should the conventional system be dropped at the time the automated system starts operating?
*Should more than one function be planned for conversion at the same time?

In banks using on-premises EDP or belonging to a joint venture, the following questions arise:

*For a given function should the center utilize existing systems and programs (canned programs) or should it write new programs based on its own needs?

In banks belonging to a joint venture, one further question arises:

*Should all the banks belonging to the center convert a given function at the same time, and if not, in what order and over what period of time?

4.6.1 Detailed Plan or the "Stepping-Stone" Approach

Only in rare cases was any specific timetable discussed during the decision period. In some cases, a general idea of the dates for conversion were given, but in others, the decision to automate was more of an approval of the idea and a specific arrangement rather than an approval of a plan and a timetable. Of course, a limiting factor for banks ordering on-premises equipment is the delivery date of the equipment, while for those using off-premises service, the timetable is frequently determined by the service provider.

Although it would be expected that a detailed timetable would be set in order to avoid the cost involved in keeping equipment idle, over half of the banks preferred not to establish such a timetable or to feel committed to one even if it was put down in writing. This was especially true among the banks that decided to convert in sections, determining the conversion date for each section only after the conversion of the previous section was successfully completed.

The establishment of a timetable is highly recommended, as it can also provide a check list for the areas to be taken care of during the conversion. The availability or lack of such a check list, outlining all the actions to be taken before and during a conversion, was a major factor in influencing the degree of success or failure of a conversion.

4.6.2 Converting by Sections or All At Once

Both approaches have their advantages and disadvantages. When a bank chooses to convert a given function by sections, the possibility of "bugs" in the program affecting the daily operations is limited to only that portion of the accounts involved. Another advantage of this approach is that the staff involved learns as it moves along with the conversion and can improve the system throughout the conversion. A disadvantage is that operations of a given function are separated into two systems which require two different staffs, or two jobs on the part of a single staff, causing problems similar to the ones evident when a parallel run is used, as discussed below.

About half of the banks chose to convert a given function all at once, while the rest converted a given function by sections, according to natural breaks in the ledger books or, in the case of banks with branches, by converting one branch at a time. No significant difference in the success of a conversion could be attributed to the approach taken by the banks on this matter, although it appears that slightly fewer problems occurred if one small section was converted first and, if successful, was followed by all other sections at once.

4.6.3 The Use of a Parallel Run

The parallel run of the old and new systems is used to check the new system for errors, permitting the old system to be utilized as a back-up if difficulties develop in the automated one. There are two major disadvantages in using a parallel run. One is that each item or document has to be processed twice. This puts time and resource pressures on the bank, especially if the conversion is of demand deposits where output is needed overnight. The second is the problem of balancing the outputs of the two systems for comparison purposes.

Of the several banks which tried to utilize the parallel run, four had to drop it within a short time because of the difficulties mentioned above. It was generally agreed among the study banks that the utility of a parallel run for more than an initial check of the output is doubtful at best.

4.6.4 How Many Functions to Convert At Once

Most of the study banks planned to automate only one function at a time. Of the eight banks which decided initially to convert more than one application, six started to plan the conversion of the second application only after they felt the first was running successfully. Only in two of the banks were two applications converted simultaneously and this was on the advice of the correspondent bank providing the service. It is recommended that banks should convert one application at a time, although a timetable for more than one can and should be set in advance as part of a long-term plan.

4.6.5 Which Bank to Convert First

In all banks belonging to a joint venture, the conversion of individual banks was done one at a time. In three cases, the bank geographically closest to the computer center was the first to be converted. As it turned out, every bank was willing to give another bank in the joint venture the honor of the first conversion and that of cleaning the "bugs" from the program. While lengthy discussions might occur in determining the order, its impact on individual EDP programs was not considered by the banks to be of major importance.

4.7 A Case of Failure

While in three of the study banks it took several weeks to overcome some serious conversion problems, in most of the others, they were solved within a few days. Only two of them experienced problems of a more serious nature, and one of the two cases is described below in order to outline some of the mistakes made before the conversion started.

The bank in question decided to use a new service bureau and attempted the first conversion only 45 days after the decision was made. Planning the conversion was left to a supervisor hired during the decision period specifically for the purpose of handling the automation program in the bank. The following interview quotes explain what happened.

The auditor of the bank described the events:

"We tried to convert all the accounts at once at the close of a business day in the middle of the week. And the next morning, after working all night, we discovered we would never be able to do it. We discovered we didn't have the appropriate forms set up and were missing the appropriate information to do such a conversion. . Our biggest discovery was that our ledger accounts were not numbered, and we had first to number them, and then plan the conversion. We had to tell the executive vice-president in the morning that we couldn't do it."

The executive vice-president, who like the auditor, had no previous EDP experience explained:

"The conversion was planned by the supervisor of demand deposits, the cashier and the auditor of the bank. I saw myself responsible for the conversion, but the work was done by my subordinates, rather than by me.

"The first time that we tried to convert was on a Wednesday afternoon, and it did not work because we had too short a time to complete the conversion. The second time, we tried to convert on a Friday afternoon, which gave us a whole weekend to get the bugs out of the operation. And the second time, we still had a lot of problems which resulted in about 40 per cent rejects and made it almost impossible to use the computer. For about a week, we were not able to return anyone's checks even if it was not covered because we feared it might be our mistake, rather than an overdrawn balance. This was the time when many in the bank suggested dropping automation altogether. But I suggested measures to move to self-posting on-premises and sent it to the computer center afterwards [parallel run]. It helped to reduce the percentage of rejects to about five per cent and a few weeks later to only two per cent."

The bookkeeping supervisor, the only person in the bank with previous EDP experience, saw it from a different point of view:

"I was very dissatisfied with the help we received from the computer center. I feel that was one of the reasons we had to do the conversion twice. I feel that some of the problems in the first conversion were a result of the initially bad system which the bank operated before the computer time. I believe that if this system would have been better, there wouldn't have been that many problems in the conversion."

The bookkeeping supervisor was not sure who the officer responsible for the conversion was. He thought it might have been the cashier, but said it was never clarified.

After the first attempt to convert failed, several officers, including the cashier and the auditor, wanted to return to the manual system and drop the EDP idea altogether. They claimed that the bank accounts were off by $6,000, although it turned out that the actual difference was closer to $100. When the senior management discovered it was possible to reduce the number of rejects and that the differences were minimal, it overruled the objections of middle management and decided to go on with the conversion.

The above quotes and other evidence point toward some of the mistakes made in this case:

*The lack of recognized authority at the top level, which would super-vise or closely follow the execution of the decision.
*The inexperience of a new person in the bank who was not familiar with this bank's operations but represented the only EDP knowledge.
*Lack of experience of the service provider.
*Lack of detailed planning of the conversion.
*Time constraint imposed by the short span of time between making the decision to automate and the first conversion.

4.8 Summary

In brief, the key to a successful conversion to EDP is planning. The probability that the problems discussed in this chapter will impair the effectiveness of the EDP system depends on the extent to which they are anticipated and provided for. The first requirement of adequate planning is time. Second, it requires painstaking analysis of the needs of the organization and its employees. Third, it must be done by people intimately familiar with banking and computer capabilities and technology. Fourth, it must be undertaken with the total support and, if possible, active participation of top management. Finally, plans should be made for the short-term (up through actual conversion) as well as the long-run, with provisions for periodic review and updating.

Included in plans formulated between the time of decision and actual conversion should be provisions for and specification of training to be given to employees at various levels and in various capacities. The more technical aspects, such as preparation of computer input and interpretation of output, are essential training, probably best accomplished on the job under the guidance of knowledgeable personnel. But basic orientation as to computer capabilities may advantageously precede the more technical training, particularly for managers and supervisors in banks planning on-premises computers, as they may participate in the design of report forms and their distribution in the system. Clerical employees should also be given basic orientation as to how the computer will operate in the bank. In this way, not only will the importance of their role be underscored but an important cause of possible resistance will be eliminated.

Chapter 5

Organizational Changes
in the Computerized Bank

In most organizations the dimensions of the organizational structure and system develop and evolve over time as a function of the way problems actually get solved in the organization. Yet it is a rare organization that takes a careful look at its system needs and then modifies its structure or methods of operations in order to better meet its needs.

One of the characteristics of an organizational system is that it tends to stabilize and resist change over time. For example, in a bank the loan officers will develop certain procedures to arrive at a loan decision based on access to given kinds of information and reports on the applicant and the reasons given for the loan application. They depend on this established procedure and over time they develop a psychological attachment to it. If anyone else in the bank wants to inquire about a specific case, he knows whom to approach and will receive a courteous response, but the information "belongs" to the loan officers. In other areas of the bank, other officers similarly control parts of the system which are relevant to their function. An effective system can develop in this manner in an organization so that everyone knows whom to approach on given matters, where to obtain relevant information and how to handle day-to-day events; everyone becomes "comfortable" in the system.

However, whenever anyone changes the system through a change in structure, operating procedure or content of information, it requires additional work on the part of all participating in the system. They must now familiarize themselves with the new "rules of the game" and possibly make adjustments in the way they were behaving in the past. It is a well-documented fact that many people resist such change.

The introduction of a computer into an organization inevitably causes changes in the total organizational system, whether they occur by design or by accident. In most organizations, the actual changes that occur will be a combination of design and accident. Mann (1955) pointed out that when a company is considering the introduction of computers, it finds itself in the rare position of being able to open up for questioning and change many long-standing and inviolable routines. This is, of course, an exceptional opportunity. It can become an occasion to reconsider both the fundamental purpose of various functions within the organization and the means by which these purposes may be achieved. Moreover, the organization is led not only to think about the reorganization of work within specific departmental or large functional areas but to redesign the entire organization, if necessary, by cutting across old departmental lines. In other words, if handled correctly, there is a psychological unfreezing of the situation, such that there are present both the logical bases and the opportunity to make changes which have long been thought desirable but which have not been made because of departmental autonomy and related historical reasons. Unfortunately, very few organizations will recognize and take advantage of the opportunity Mann describes.

This chapter will review some of the changes that are occurring in the organizational system as a result of the computer. The discussion will focus on three specific areas:

Developments in the information system of the bank from two points of view: its content and process. In the area of content, the discussion will focus on *what* is being transmitted and in the area of process, it will focus on *how* it is being transmitted. The ultimate effectiveness of any information system is a function of the interaction between these two variables. In other words, it is not enough for an organization to have available the right information; it must also provide for the means of communicating this information to the right people at the right time.

The effects of the computer on decision-making prerogatives and the loci of decision-making within the organization. The discussion will consider the changes in managerial decision-making activities as a result of changes in the content and process of the information system.

Changes in the functional structure of the organization. Here issues of authority and functional responsibility, communication and coordination, supervision and control will be related to present and future changes resulting from the introduction of EDP.

The conclusion of the chapter will evaluate the necessity for a modified organizational system in view of the results of the study and developments in information technology.

5.1 Developing an Information System

A computer adds a new dimension to an organization's information system in terms of what is possible. That is, once a given amount of raw data is encoded and available on the computer, many analyses can be performed on the data and a great number of reports can be generated. Some of these are simple and inexpensive to produce and others are complex and costly in terms of the time, money and man-hours required to develop and produce them. Every organization must set priorities on the number, form and content of the reports to be produced, since they will not be able to print out everything desired by all managers. (If they could, it would likely inundate the organization in paper.) As a result, the control of the content, amount of information processed and means of transmitting it throughout the organization are likely to emerge as significant problems.

5.1.1 Basic Data Processing

The use of a computer in the study banks has enabled them to make a significant improvement in their basic record keeping or data processing, including both the speed and accuracy of same. This is the most predominant benefit which banking officers ascribe to the computer. The specific area in which this benefit is realized varies from one bank to another depending upon their primary activity or orientation. For the large majority of banks, however, it is realized in the area of demand deposit accounting. Bankers are relieved of the need to maintain a set of posting machines and a staff of skilled bookkeepers. The possibility for human error in calculating and summarizing has been reduced considerably.

The traditional bookkeeping job was a boring one so that competent personnel were difficult to obtain and turnover was high. In addition, overtime was frequently required so that this entire area often developed into a persistent headache for a bank. Automation does not completely solve the problem; for example, there is still the boring job of filing checks. However, it does reduce the personnel problem and at the same time permits substantial increases in volume with very little additional personnel required.

5.1.2 The Input Process

Whether the computer is going to be utilized for basic data processing or for more sophisticated management science applications, one of the key factors in successful operations remains the input process. The computer can be programmed to audit and reject certain types of input, but in many cases it will simply process it and the result is faulty output. Even when the computer does catch input errors and rejects them, there are costs involved in the slowdown of processing operations and the need to correct the errors.

Inaccurate input is especially dangerous because of the tendency of many people to accept printed output as proofed evidence. Many who would check the reliability of a handwritten accounting sheet, will fail to do so if it is printed by the computer. One way to remedy such a tendency is to educate the users of the output. At the same time, it is necessary to make every effort to reduce to a minimum the number of input errors.

In a majority of the banks studied, there was a feeling that preparing input would be easier and more effective if the computer was on-premises. However, observations indicate that when the computer is on-premises there is a more relaxed attitude toward preparing input and the net result is that it usually takes more time with more slack in the system. The attitude of "After all, if one makes an error in input, the computer is right in the building and it is easy to correct" frequently leads to considerable inefficiency in preparing input. Moreover, the system for preparing computer input was usually more organized and more effective in a service bureau operation or a correspondent situation than in an on-premises center.

Table 5.1

THE EXTENT TO WHICH THE RESPONDENT HAS
OBSERVED ERRORS IN PREPARATION OF MATERIAL
FOR THE COMPUTER AS A PROBLEM IN HIS BANK

		Degree of problem (percentage)		
Type EDP arrangement	N	Little or no problem	Problem to some extent	Serious problem
On-premises EDP	183	43.2	45.3	11.5
Joint venture or holding co.	96	49.0	42.7	8.3
Service bureau or another bank	140	63.6	32.1	4.3
Total	419	51.3	40.3	8.4

The data in Table 5.1 support the interview results. Almost 57 per cent of the respondents in the banks having their own EDP equipment saw input preparation as a problem, compared to slightly less than 37 per cent holding the same view in the banks using a service bureau or another bank's computer. The banks belonging to a joint venture or using holding company EDP are in between the other two groups (51 per cent). There the complaint often evolved around the lack of training and insufficient control over the input process.

Looking at attitudes towards input preparation as a function of age, 69 per cent of the age group 30 and below felt that preparing computer input was not a greater job than the prior accounting work. In the 31-58 year-old age groups, 55 per cent expressed this attitude and in the age group 58 and over only 45 per cent expressed it. There is no question of the existence of a halo effect operating in the expression of these attitudes. That is, the older managers have a greater tendency to resist change than do the younger age groups and this influences many of their attitudes towards EDP. One of the ways in which this is evidenced is their consistent devaluation of the accomplishments of the computer along with a persistent overemphasis on the problems experienced with the computer. The younger age group, on the other hand, reacts strongly in the opposite direction. They are more likely to emphasize one or two accomplishments of the computer and then ignore or minimize the significance of problems which are associated with it.

5.1.3 Content and Format of Reports

Use of a computer has enabled many banks to retrieve in report form considerable information which always existed but was too costly or impractical to process on a regular basis. Examples are the average balance report, significant balance change, daily overdraft and activity reports, all of which present "new" information as regular periodical reports. In the study banks there was considerable uniformity of reports from one bank to another regardless of the type of automation program in use. This is no doubt due in part to the high degree of similarity in the functions performed by the banks. However, it may also be a commentary on the lack of real innovation in this area.[1]

An interesting paradox emerged from our interviews with banking officers regarding the nature and utilization of computer output. The large majority felt that it represented a significant improvement over the pre-computer reports, but at the same time they felt quite strongly that they were not making full use of the information. (There was only a small minority, mostly older officers, who expressed a preference for the old bookkeeping system.)

In many banks, there were one or two reports which were singled out by a senior officer as being more important than the others, and as a result, their

---

[1] Appendix C shows a typical list of reports in the three most automated areas: demand deposit accounting, savings and installment loans.

worth relative to all the others was overemphasized. For example, if the president looked at only two reports daily, the overdraft report and the report of significant balance change, then other officers were likely to do the same, often neglecting other useful reports.

Looking at attitudes towards computer output as a function of the form of automation program being used in the bank, one can see that in general, those banks using a service computer or having a computer on-premises are most positive about computer output, and those participating in a joint venture or being serviced by their holding company are most negative. Looking first at the responses to the first item in Table 5.2, one can see the trend described above quite clearly. Of the respondents, 61 per cent in banks using their own computer or a service bureau felt that the computer output was easier to understand than the old ledger and filing systems, whereas only 47 per cent of those in joint ventures and 42 per cent using a holding company felt this way.

Table 5.2

ATTITUDES TOWARD COMPUTER OUTPUT AS A
FUNCTION OF FORM OF AUTOMATION

			Per cent responding		
Item	*Form of automation*	*N*	*Agree*	*Don't know*	*Disagree*
Computer output is easier to understand than the old ledger and filing systems.	On-premises	186	61	7	32
	Service bureau	43	61	5	35
	Correspondent	105	53	7	39
	Joint venture	51	47	10	43
	Holding company	53	42	6	51
	Total	438	55	7	38
The reports I now get from the computer represent a vast improvement with regard to the amount and kind of information I (or someone in the position I now occupy) got before EDP.	On-premises	186	81	8	9
	Service bureau	43	88	2	9
	Correspondent	105	87	6	6
	Joint venture	51	75	4	22
	Holding company	53	79	6	13
	Total	438	82	6	10
In general, computers produce only standard reports which are not helpful to me in making specific decisions.	On-premises	186	17	5	77
	Service bureau	43	16	0	84
	Correspondent	105	22	5	72
	Joint venture	51	33	8	59
	Holding company	53	34	6	59
	Total	438	22	5	72

By and large there was nothing complex or difficult to understand in the computer output referred to above. As to those fairly large groups in each category who say computer output is *not* as easy to understand as the old system, this is simply one reasonably inoffensive way in which officers can express their resistance to automation. In other words, some officers who have lost their familiar reports and to some extent their control over reports, do not *want* to find it easy to understand computer output—so they simply do not.

On items aimed directly at assessing the quality of the information, this trend continues. A higher per cent of those having a computer on-premises, or using a service bureau or a correspondent, felt that use of a computer had improved significantly the quality of information than did those in banks using a holding company computer or participating in a joint venture. It is interesting and informative that those using a service bureau are just as positive about the computer output they are now receiving as those using an on-premises computer, and those using a correspondent service are not far behind them. This would seem to indicate that it is feasible to send items out for processing and still have an effective automation program if the service provider is interested in your account and willing to invest in the necessary programming.

The same data, broken down on the basis of whether or not the respondents receive computer output, provide evidence for the thesis that people develop firm attitudes even in the absence of real knowledge or information about a given subject. (See Table 5.3.) In all likelihood, those respondents who do not receive computer output on a regular basis have no first-hand knowledge of the usefulness of the information. Nevertheless, the large majority of them develop some attitudes as a consequence of interacting with those in the bank who do receive the output. The negative attitudes on the part of those who do not receive the output may be due to a feeling of being left out of the mainstream of the information flow of the bank. Alternately, it may mean that those persons receiving output who are negative about it are more vocal and therefore have a great influence on those not receiving it.

The last reason advanced is quite plausible in the light of much of our interview experience. For example, in close to 80 per cent of the banks visited, at least one officer was not happy with the automation program. Typically, such a person misses the ledger card system which he had before the use of computers and simply refuses to give it up. Such a person is likely to make more noise about his dissatisfaction than other officers who are quite content with the automated system.

In some banks we found ourselves sympathizing with these officers. In one bank, for example, where delinquencies were a problem, a senior loan officer complained about the pure objectivity of the computer and the difficulty of making exceptions in the loan area. In the past, he had treated delinquents on an individual basis. There were and still are occasions on which some of his best customers are unable to meet a payment for an accepted reason. When a manual system of posting was used, and all the information on a given loan was contained on a ledger card, it was easy for him to review the card and indicate an exception, that is, a late payment, right on the card before a past-due notice was mailed to the customer. With their computer program, however, the computer indicates a delinquency immediately when a loan is even one day late, and this delinquency can subsequently affect a person's credit rating. Another problem the same loan officer cited was that if a man owing $85.09 sent a check for $85.00 even, the computer would automatically consider him delinquent, whereas the bank considers this to be a reasonable payment and would ordinarily give the man the benefit of the doubt and apply the nine cents to next month's bill.

Table 5.3

ATTITUDES TOWARDS COMPUTER OUTPUT OF THOSE
WHO RECEIVE COMPUTER OUTPUT ON A REGULAR
BASIS COMPARED TO THOSE WHO DO NOT

| | | | Per cent responding | | |
Item	*Receive output*	*N*	*Agree*	*Don't know*	*Disagree*
The reports I now get from	Yes	316	89	4	7
the computer represent a vast	No	107	64	15	17
improvement with regard to	Total	423	82	6	10
the amount and kind of infor-					
mation I (or someone in the					
position I now occupy) got					
before EDP.					
In general, computers produce	Yes	316	19	3	79
only standard reports which	No	107	30	13	54
are not helpful to me in making	Total	423	22	5	72
specific decisions.					

Officers under such a program of automation have a legitimate complaint. It was aptly demonstrated in other study banks that it is by no means necessary to build such rigidity into a computer program. For example, one of our study banks had its installment loan program so designed that a payment of at least 70 per cent of the total amount due was not considered delinquent. In such cases, the computer automatically updates and adjusts the amount still owed on an account. (In addition, the computer program automatically adds late charges onto such an account, and the income from this has proven to be fairly substantial.) The flexibility of this program has in fact been an effective selling point to customers and has saved the bank a great many headaches. A customer, for example, can pay a little bit less one month and catch up the following month, or he can liquidate himself sooner by constantly paying a little more than is due.

The halo effect described earlier in relation to the age of respondents can also be seen in the responses to the items now under discussion. Of those 30 years old and under, 76 per cent felt that automation had improved the quality of information quite a bit; in the next age group (31-44) this percentage dropped to 72; in the next (45-58) it dropped to 70; and in the 58 and over category, the percentage was 68. This same trend was found in an earlier study of a large metropolitan area bank (Vaughan and Porat, 1967); there the older officers consistently underestimated the impact of computers and the younger officers tended to overestimate it.

The formation of these attitudes may be influenced to a considerable degree by the frequent magazine articles describing how the computer will take over or change many management jobs. The middle age group, with several years of work remaining and with no real basis on which to evaluate these articles, quite naturally is concerned and would like to believe that they are not true. The younger age group, on the other hand, has a great deal more room for optimism. Many of this group have been exposed to computers during their college days and therefore have a leg up on the older group of managers in this area. They reason that the jobs which will be done away with are those occupied by the older managers and they therefore feel that they are in a favorable position to compete for the jobs that will be left. Both points of view are very understandable, albeit a little out of touch with what is actually happening.

5.1.4 Utilization of Computer Output

When asked specifically about the relevance of automated information for serving customers, the response was similar to that described above about general information from the computer. Those respondents whose banks have a computer on-premises or are served by a service bureau or correspondent are significantly more positive in their attitudes than those whose banks are participating in a joint venture or are served by a holding company computer. The differences here are even more pronounced, in fact, than those discussed earlier. (See Table 5.4.)

Figure 5.1 shows a graphic display of the responses to the same item as a function of age. The effect of age in this area is much more dramatic than in the area of general information. This is due in part to the fact that the older banking officer has long-established customer relationships and operates with a concept of personal service to these customers. Even though a considerable number of this older age group perceive that on balance the computer is doing a good job in processing information, they cannot resist venting their dissatisfaction with the impersonal aspects of computer operations. The younger officers, on the other hand, have more of a mass market orientation. They typically have not been in the bank long enough to establish close personal relationships with customers so that they have had to give up very little in this regard. At the same time, they appreciate the tremendous advantage that the computer provides when responding to the masses.

Table 5.4

ATTITUDES TOWARDS UTILITY OF COMPUTER OUTPUT
FOR SERVING CUSTOMERS

			Per cent responding		
Item	Form of Automation	N	Agree	Don't know	Disagree
The computer has enabled	On-premises	186	83	2	15
us to respond more quickly	Service bureau	43	88	2	9
to customer needs and	Correspondent	105	76	7	16
requests	Holding company	53	66	2	29
	Joint venture	51	57	8	33
	Total	438	77	4	19

Overall, managers feel they make good use of the output they receive. Of the total sample, 57 per cent felt that computer reports were being used in an optimally effective way by management, while only 27 per cent disagreed with this notion. Looking at the responses to this issue as a function of age, it is not surprising to find that the youngest age groups were most critical of management's use of reports. This is due in part to the very common feeling on the parts of younger officers that they could do a better job of using the reports than the older managers who are, of course, in the majority. At the same time, it is likely that the younger managers are more in tune with the potential of computer reports and thus are more critical of management's failure to realize the potential.

FIGURE 5.1 RESPONSES TO THE STATEMENT:
THE COMPUTER HAS ENABLED US TO RESPOND MORE QUICKLY TO
CUSTOMER NEEDS AND REQUESTS

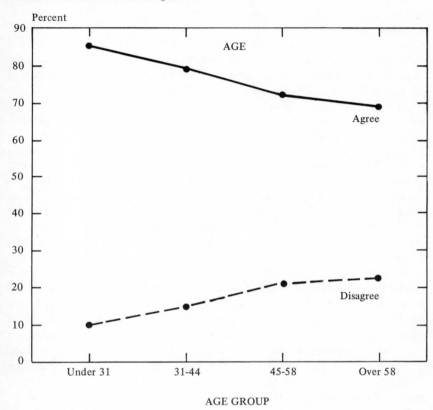

5.2 The Effect of the Computer on Decision-Making

One of the major roles attributed to the computer over the last decade is that of improving management decision-making. The supplying of more information faster and in a new, easy-to-follow format should have freed the manager from the time-consuming need to assemble and summarize data and permit him to do more analysis and interpretation of the data. For the most part, the happy day when this will materialize organization-wide is still ahead of us. We have already noted that the study banks have used the computer primarily for simple data processing tasks and have paid little attention to its use as a decision-making tool. Yet some effects on decision-making are already evident as second-order benefits of improved data processing.

The perceived role of the computer in decision-making to date is reflected in the responses given by the managers to the statement: "The computer is currently playing a major role in managerial decision-making in our bank." Only one-fourth of the total sample agreed with the statement, while 60 per cent disagreed. The per cent of those agreeing was especially high among the chief executive officers (37 per cent) and those responsible for the processing of the work, i.e., EDP operations (39 per cent) and bookkeeping (35 per cent). The operations people are presenting their bias here toward the importance of their role, while the chief executives are probably expressing wishful thinking that other officers are actually being influenced by the computer output.

As EDP experience increases, more officers feel that the computer is playing a major role in managerial decision-making in their banks. This is a direct result of increased use of computer output and, in some cases, of improved content of the information supplied. The per cent of those agreeing that the computer is currently playing a major role in decision-making in their bank is twice as much in those banks having used EDP for more than 4 years (33 per cent) compared to those using it under 2 years (17 per cent).

While the majority of respondents do not feel that the computer is currently playing a *major* role in decision-making, 75 per cent believe it has made possible *better* management decision-making. (See Figure 5.3.) This happened mainly as a result of freeing the manager from many of the chores of supervising and administrating routine paper work. In addition, more accurate and timely information and the more readable format of data presentation are now available. Over time the use of this information increases the feeling that the computer helps management considerably in making better decisions. At the same time, observations show that the use of information, even if readily available, is still limited and has yet to be "discovered" by many officers.

5.2.1 Level of Decision-Making

The great majority of respondents (75 per cent) felt that the introduction of the computer had not changed the hierarchical level at which decisions are made in the bank. The remaining officers were about equally divided between those who felt day-to-day decisions are made now at lower levels and those who felt they are made at higher levels. It is difficult to generalize about this issue in banking as a whole, as it depends on the type of decision and the management practices in the specific bank.

With more timely output available for the lower levels, it is possible to

FIGURE 5.2 PERCENT RESPONSES TO THE STATEMENT:
THE COMPUTER IS CURRENTLY PLAYING A MAJOR ROLE IN MANAGERIAL
DECISION-MAKING IN OUR BANK.

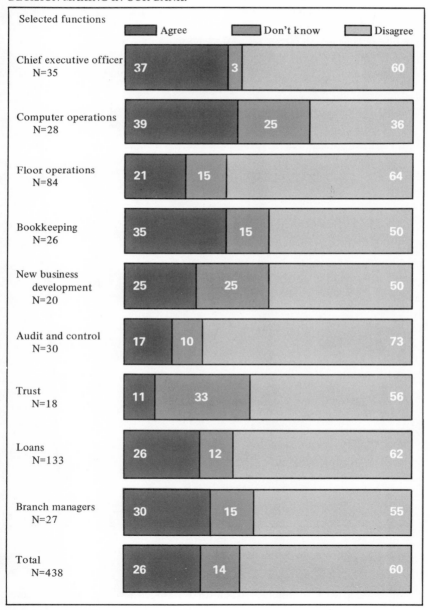

establish guidelines which will permit employees at that level to make more decisions on the spot. At the same time, however, the availability of summary reports will allow top management in some banks to be better informed about daily operations. In a small organization this might result in more participation of the top echelon in day-to-day work, especially if the person at a higher level is interested in centralization and keeping an eye on details. In the final analysis, the computer will facilitate the movement of decision-making either upward or downward, but top management will decide which way according to its own preferences.

FIGURE 5.3 EVALUATION OF THE DEGREE TO WHICH THE COMPUTER'
HAS MADE POSSIBLE BETTER MANAGEMENT DECISION-MAKING
IN THE RESPONDENT'S BANK.

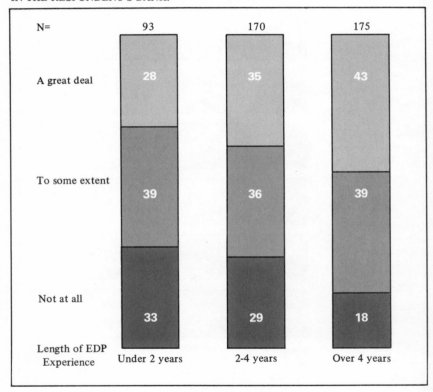

*5.2.2 Effects on the Scope of
       Decision-Making*

Interesting patterns emerged when the respondents were asked to estimate the effect of the computer on the scope of decision-making with reference to themselves, their boss, and their subordinates. When asked how the computer had affected the range of their decision-making, only a small minority (2 per cent) said it had restricted their range of decision-making, while 35 per cent felt it had increased it. More officers, regardless of level in the organization, felt it had increased the range for their boss or subordinates.

Breaking this down by functions (see Figure 5.4), managers in computer operations felt most strongly that they and their bosses have greater decision-making discretion because of the computer. This is not surprising, but the following response is. Bookkeepers also felt strongly that they are able to make more day-to-day decisions now than in the pre-computer period.

Chief executive officers were the only group to indicate that their subordinates now make more decisions than they themselves do as a function of the computer. This may be due to a feeling that they can delegate more since subordinates now have more information available for making decisions, or it may be that the computer has increased the structure of decision-making to an extent where they feel able to sit back and supervise through computer reports.

Loan officers present a unique picture. They feel less strongly than any other group that their decision-making scope has increased. On the basis of interviews these results were expected. The majority of loan officers interviewed felt that their decisions were hampered by the computer, as they no longer had the ledger cards to show them an historical picture of an account to be used as a basis for a loan decision. This does not suggest that they necessarily have negative attitudes toward the use of the computer in the loan area in general but only that they are not completely happy with the trade-off in which they get more accurate summary information more quickly in exchange for the loss of the immediately available historical record.

The longer a manager has been in banking, the less likely he is to agree that the computer has increased the range of decision-making for himself, his subordinates and his boss. (See Figure 5.5.) As age is highly correlated with length of banking experience, this result is not surprising. Before writing the older age group off as being out-of-touch, one should consider that older managers often have a deeper understanding of the fundamental qualitative nature of many banking decisions and thus may believe quite correctly that computers will always be an adjunct dealing with the fringes of decisions which are crucial to the long-term viability of the bank. Those in banking less than five years have probably witnessed the conversion to computer and were overly impressed with the changes that did occur.

Only one-fourth of the managers felt the computer had increased the visibility of the decisions they make. This result is much lower than was found in larger banks and is probably due to one chief reason. Our study banks were relatively small in size and number of personnel, and even before

FIGURE 5.4 PERCENT OF BANK MANAGERS, BY FUNCTION, WHO FEEL THE COMPUTER HAS INCREASED THE RANGE OF DECISION-MAKING FOR THEIR SUBORDINATES, THEMSELVES AND THEIR BOSS.

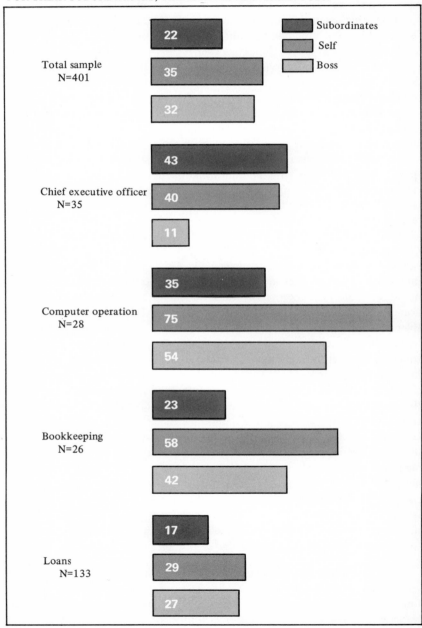

FIGURE 5.5 PERCENT OF BANK MANAGERS, BY LENGTH OF TIME
IN THE BANKING INDUSTRY, WHO FEEL THE COMPUTER HAS
INCREASED THE RANGE OF DECISION-MAKING FOR THEIR
SUBORDINATES, THEMSELVES AND THEIR BOSS.

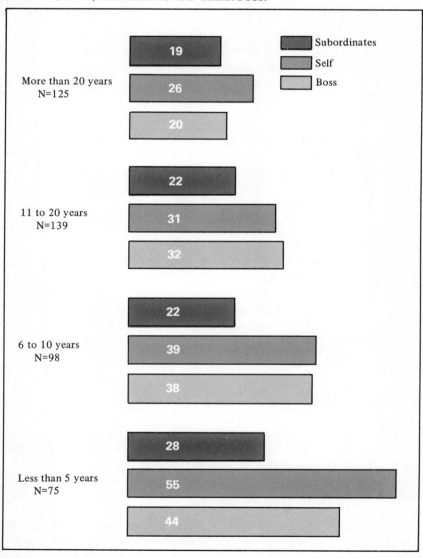

the computer, decisions were more visible than in large organizations. For
example, in large banks, computerization of loans means a drastic change,

where all loans made in the previous day can now be reviewed by supervisors on the spot without the loan officers even knowing it. At the same time, in many small banks loan officer reports were scheduled daily even before the computer arrived, so that visibility was not significantly changed after conversion. The increased visibility was expressed mostly by the computer people, bookkeeping officers and chief executives who now have a chance to review output regularly and are much more aware of the possibilities for checking on others in the bank, compared to the other officers.

5.2.3 Long-Term Effects on Decision-Making

Although at present the role of the computer in decision-making in banks, especially the smaller ones, is still felt to be quite limited, 56 per cent of the respondents believe that in the next 10-15 years many of the decisions made currently by management will be made by the computer. Only 37 per cent disagree with this. Thus, by and large, bank managers are cognizant of the greater impact still to be realized in using computers in decision-making. A greater percentage of people involved in computer operations agree with this statement (71 per cent) than is true for any other group. Those who agree least with the statement are the branch managers, who at present have too little contact with the computer to be able to evaluate its future role. The per cent of those agreeing with the statement increases with the length of time the bank has been using EDP. While only 48 per cent of those having the computer less than 2 years agreed with the statement, 59 per cent of those with over 2 years' experience agreed with it.

5.3 Changes in the Functional Structure

Earlier we mentioned the opportunity a bank has when it introduces an automation program in terms of reviewing and possibly changing functional responsibilities and traditional modes of operating. As it was pointed out, none of the study banks took the opportunity to plan the change and thus it occurred sporadically. The computer manager and his staff in an on-premises situation may assume important roles as change agents in such cases where the organization has not formally delegated this responsibility. (See Chapter 6.) Whether they realize it or not, they are sitting in a seat with considerable power and potential influence because of their specialized knowledge and day-to-day control over information processing. Some do perceive this quite clearly and proceed with their own "program" of organizational change. The person or persons who serve as liaison between the bank and a service center in an off-premises arrangement have similar power to control and manipulate the flow of information but not nearly as much as their counterparts in an on-premises center.

5.3.1 Authority and Functional Responsibility

In the large banks it was observed that over time the computer does change the lines of informal authority even if the formal acknowledgements of such changes are slow to follow (Vaughan and Porat, 1967). No such changes can be expected in the small to medium-sized bank for the following reason. In those banks the hierarchy usually involves only three or four layers of authority from the top executive to the level of non-management employees. Typically, lines of authority are relatively fluid in that a few senior officers are likely to make all the major decisions and singly or as a group get involved in any kind of problem at any level in the organization with the possible exception of the very lowest level. Given the relatively small size of the organization and the accompanying ease of working in this fluid manner, we would not expect the computer to change significantly the formal lines of authority in the bank.

At the same time, the computer is apt to affect the dimensions of functional responsibility. When asked whether the computer was breaking down previously clear areas of functional responsibility, half the respondents indicated that it was not, and a fairly sizeable group (30 per cent) felt that it was. Bookkeeping supervisors were most ambivalent in their responses to this item, indicating that there still exists some confusion about their new role as intermediary between the EDP function and other sections in the bank. Twenty-seven per cent said they did not know and the remainder were almost equally split over the issue. Their function in the bank has changed considerably; in fact, it is probably the most affected job in the bank. They must be familiar with all computer-related aspects of their subordinates' jobs and are now charged with examining the accuracy of computer output and transmitting it to other departments.

Among managers of floor operations, 36 per cent feel less clear than before about their areas of responsibility. In banks using off-premises computer servicing, they are the most likely candidates outside of bookkeeping to be responsible for EDP and to serve as the liaison with the computer operation. Not having been trained in the EDP area they, like the bookkeeping officers, often experience considerable frustration in their role as men-in-the-middle, caught between their managers' needs and the computer center's requirements and available means for satisfying those needs. Also, with the concentration of the processing function in the EDP department, many floor officers feel they have lost touch with this part of the operation. On the other hand, computer managers are the least likely to say that functional responsibilities are changing as a consequence of automation. This would seem to be more of a guarded response than their real feeling about the matter.

5.3.2 Patterns of Coordination and Personnel Communication

The two groups who are experiencing the most change in patterns of communication are the bookkeeping group and those with some direct responsibility for the computer operation. Whether or not these two groups communicate more or less with their bosses and other officers is a direct function of the effectiveness of their automation program. Effectiveness as referred to here is the extent to which the program is relatively bug-free and the extent to which the officers in the bank perceive the information they are getting to be adequate.

In banks where the automation program is relatively effective, there seems to have been a decrease in the amount of communication between the two aforementioned groups and the other officers in the bank. The reasons seem to be twofold. First, there is not the need for communication which existed earlier as long as the computer output furnishes officers with the necessary information in a readable and understandable format. Second, there is not as much basis for communication as existed prior to the computer. That is, the other officers do not understand what the computing group and the bookkeeping group are about, so they cannot ask as many questions or communicate about as many matters as they could when the bank was on a manual system with which they had literally grown up. In banks where the automation program is relatively ineffective there seems to have been an increase in the amount of communication. That is, in situations where computer reports are incomplete or inaccurate, the officers must constantly query the bookkeeping department and the computer operation in order to obtain the information they need. As one would expect, such an increase in communications usually has a negative effect.

At the same time, the computer is having relatively little effect on the communication patterns of the officers as a whole. In most banks, there is a small group of senior officers, usually three or four, who control the critical information in the bank and make all the major decisions. This pattern does not seem to be changing at this time. However, many officers at lower levels of the bank perceive that it has changed or is in the process of changing.

One of the reasons for change in communication patterns is associated with the need to increase or decrease coordination within the bank. Bookkeeping supervisors, as expected from previous discussions, did not feel that coordination problems have decreased as much as did the sample as a whole. This reflects the fact that the exact nature of their redefined role in the bank's functioning has not yet stabilized. By way of contrast, branch managers perceive a much greater decrease in such problems than does the average manager. Prior to the introduction of the computer, when records were kept in individual branches and bookkeeping was done in the branch, coordination between the branches and the main office was extremely difficult. A customer wishing to transact business usually had to go to the particular branch that had his account or else be subjected to a considerable delay while phone calls were made to check the status of his account. Since the computer was introduced, the great majority of banks have all their records kept at the main office, eliminating the need for branch bookkeeping and record-keeping. Each account has a branch code, so that if a question arises a short phone call to a central location or the use of a central display system supplies the answer. As a result of this easier access to information, branch managers often find it much easier coordinating with other branches and the main office.

5.3.3 Control and Supervision

Tied in with the effect of the computer on intra-organization coordination is its impact on control of operations. As might be expected, computer managers feel quite strongly that the computer permits a better grasp of the entire bank's activities and therefore better management control over the operations. (See Table 5.5.) This view is held to an even greater extent by chief executive officers. Not a single one of the latter group expressed an opposing position. The bookkeeping officers are the only ones with any sizeable per cent disagreeing with the above, and this is no doubt due to the lingering confusion in their jobs described above. Field interviews lend support to this overall positive feeling of increased control due to automation. More accurate and timely reports along with some new information are credited for making the chief difference.

As can be seen in Table 5.5, control improves with length of experience with computers. Only 30 per cent of those using computers for less than 2 years felt strongly that the computer helped considerably in controlling operations, whereas 47 per cent of those with 4 years of experience expressed this opinion. As managers get used to living with any system or set of procedures, they feel more comfortable with it and are able to utilize it more effectively. At the same time, there is little doubt that better control can and will be achieved as the computer comes to be viewed as more than just a fast bookkeeping machine.

As one would expect, managers who receive output from the computer feel more strongly than those who do not, that management has better control over bank operations. This is due to the fact that they now have more timely information available to them that can be used for control purposes. Two examples, observed in the present study, of the possible use of EDP for better performance control in the loan area are outlined below.

Table 5.5

RESPONSES TO THE QUESTION: HAS THE COMPUTER
HELPED TO CONTROL OPERATIONS?

		Per cent responding			
Function	N	Quite a bit	Somewhat	Not at all	Not applicable to my job
Branch managers	27	37	48	4	11
Chief executive officers	35	59	41	0	0
Computer operations managers	28	54	39	0	8
Floor operations managers	84	40	43	5	12
Bookkeeping supervisors	26	44	28	12	16
Length of EDP experience					
Less than 2 years	93	30	42	5	24
2 to 4 years	170	39	43	4	15
More than 4 years	175	47	36	5	12
Access to EDP output					
Receives output	316	44	41	4	12
Receives no output	107	29	35	7	29
Total	438	40	40	5	15

In one bank the chief executive officer and chief loan officer received a monthly computer report of the number, types and amounts of loans made by each loan officer. At regular intervals each loan officer sat down with the chief loan officer and made specific projections as to his expected monthly performance over the next time period. Then his actual versus his expected performance was charted each month and was available for all officers to see. The computer made it possible to calculate individual profitability for each officer, thus increasing the meaningfulness of the data. Results were reviewed and new projections made each month by the chief loan officer together with each individual loan officer. Prizes were given for highest volume and best forecasts. The plan was self-motivating and actually reduced the need for human supervision.

Another bank had the same kind of computer report on loan officers' performance but kept it between the chief executive officer and chief loan officer without making it available to other loan officers. The two men would review the report monthly; when a particular officer's performance was substandard, they would discuss the matter with the officer concerned. Thus, the computer permitted management to monitor performance in a way that was not practical prior to the advent of automation. However, we would predict that this method of using the information will not prove to be as effective and acceptable to the loan officers as that described in the first example.

5.4 Organizational Systems and Computer Technology—A Summary

The introduction of a computer in the bank begins an evolutionary process which has several identifiable stages. The first stage is that of automating the basic data processing. The large majority of banks are still in this first stage. The second state involves changes in the kinds of information which are available for decision-making and the way in which the information is used. Only a few of the study banks were just beginning to scratch the surface of this stage. The third is the development of new management techniques and re-structuring of the decision-making processes. None of the study banks were at this stage or anticipated reaching it in the short-run.

In a real sense, the success or failure of an automation program in the first two phases is dependent on the readability and general effectiveness of the reports it generates. One cannot overstress the importance of format and readability. A good report not only contains all the needed information; it contains it in a form which is easy for the manager to understand and does not require that he dig through 20 pages of computer output in order to extract five or six pieces of information.

Many of the banks using an off-premises service have presently no choice as to the nature of the reports they receive. They must simply accept those generated from a canned program previously developed by the service center or a correspondent bank. Nevertheless, much of the survey data would indicate that the reports provided by service centers or correspondents are certainly as effective or at least as well accepted as those generated in on-premises situations.

Banks which have their own computer on-premises still have their share of problems in this area. It is our observation that most bank officers are not particularly cognizant of the need for constant improvement of the information they want. Only a few of them actually generate meaningful requests for new or modified types of reports. As a result, the task of modifying the content and form of presentation of information is left to the EDP people, who often do not understand what the bank officer really needs. They should, of course, have a voice in determining the ultimate form and application the related reports take; however, their desires must sometimes be compromised with the capabilities of their computer system, the time of their computer personnel, and the cost involved. What is needed is a very careful analysis of the information used and needed by management at the time an application is being programmed and then periodic checks to see if reports are providing the necessary information, if they need to be modified, or if they can be discontinued because of lack of use.

Following is a brief summary of the experience to date:

*The introduction of a computer into a bank inevitably causes changes, either intentional or accidental, in the "content and process" of the information system. The ultimate effectiveness of any information system is a function of the interaction between these two variables. In other words, it is not enough for an organization to have available the right information (content); it must also provide the means of communicating this information to the right people at the right time (process).

*A substantial majority of bank officers feel that the computer has enabled them to give better service to customers. At the same time the majority also recognize that they are not making maximum use of computer reports, with the youngest age group being most critical in this regard.

*The technology exists now for a bank to make significant improvements in its information system, and the introduction of a computer provides a unique opportunity for the instigation of change.

*Bank managers believe that while the computer does not currently play a major role in decision-making, it is likely to do so in the future. The longer a bank's experience with EDP, the greater its managers feel its present impact to be and the greater they predict the future role will be in decision-making.

*In the short run, managers feel that decisions are made at the same levels of the organization as they were before the computer was introduced. However, it appears that the kinds of decisions made at each level are changing, and top management should be aware of the consequences such a trend has on management development and task allocations.

*Computer impact on the communication patterns depends in the main on the perceived effectiveness of automation; "felt effectiveness" is likely to decrease the amount of communication between top management and the remaining officers and "felt ineffectiveness" is likely to increase it.

*In terms of procedures, the bookkeeping group is the most uncertain, in the short run, about its new function and responsibilities. One consequence is the feeling that coordination has become more difficult for them while coordination problems are being reduced at the branch manager's level.

*The introduction of the computer often causes a feeling of loss of authority and responsibility—especially at the branch and lower management levels. By providing a central focus for the bank's operations, the computer can give to management a better grasp of what is happening in the bank, and consequently, better overall control. The prevalence of this feeling increases with the length of time a bank has used EDP.

Chapter 6

The Computer
and the Banker's Job

Every organization introducing a technological innovation as significant as EDP can expect to face some negative attitudes or resistance among its employees. Moreover, the computer seems to generate more than average resistance because of the tremendous power attributed to it, the lack of any previous familiarity with this kind of machine, and the wide coverage in the popular and professional news media of its impact on people and jobs. It takes considerable time to change an organizational system or structure and even when changes do occur it is sometimes difficult to identify them in the short run. At the same time, the individual job holder is much quicker to sense the impact of a change on his own position. Even before he thinks consciously about the actual effects of the change he develops attitudes and perceptions toward it and the people associated with the change.

This chapter will focus on three areas directly related to the individual job holder. First, the impact EDP has had on job content and the skill requirements needed to fulfill managerial jobs in a computerized bank will be reviewed. Second, management's attitudes toward one specific job group will be examined. That group consists of the computer personnel, including those who manage the computer in an on-premises type of arrangement and those responsible for coordinating the EDP activities in an off-premises arrangement.

Third, the subject of future personnel advancement within the organization will be examined. Here consideration will be given to the effect that changes in the number of jobs, skill requirements and the entry of the computer staff into the organization have had on staff promotion in the long and short-run.

6.1 Changes in Skill Requirements

Throughout the book it has been emphasized that the major effects of the computer are still to be felt by most banks, including those which have automated within recent years. Nevertheless, even though its function in many organizations has been primarily that of a high-speed bookkeeping device, it has caused changes in job content and also in skill requirements. For example, the majority of the respondents (58 per cent) felt that the computer has made their overall job easier, while 24 per cent felt the computer had not helped in this regard. (See Figure 6.1.) The results become even more significant when only the responses of those who receive EDP output on a regular basis are considered. In this group, 65 per cent of the respondents felt EDP has made their overall job easier. (Among bookkeeping managers, 81 per cent expressed the same opinion.)

If the computer is being used effectively, one's job may be "easier" in the sense that more accurate information is now produced more quickly by a machine, whereas prior to the introduction of the computer, gathering such information was often too time consuming to be worthwhile. Theoretically, a manager's time is more profitably spent if he is evaluating information provided by someone else rather than collecting the information himself. However, creative use of the computer-generated information does not occur automatically and, in fact, will probably require additional training and considerable experience before it is achieved.

The impact of the computer is seen also in the need for new and upgraded skills. A majority of respondents felt that skills have been upgraded at all levels as a function of automation, with the greatest percentage (67) expressing this perception about the supervisory level than any other level. (See Table 6.1.) The only negative perception of any magnitude in this area was with regard to the lower level, where 15 per cent felt that clerical jobs had actually been downgraded with respect to skills required. For the most part, these results support our observations that most jobs have been upgraded, if affected at all, and that the most noticeable need for new skills and knowledge is seen at the supervisory level where the responsibility for day-to-day operation lies. For some of the clerical functions such as in data processing, there has not been any noticeable downgrading in skills; in other jobs such as that of a check filer, the job has been simplified considerably,

FIGURE 6.1 PERCENT RESPONSES TO THE QUESTION:
"HAS THE INTRODUCTION OF THE COMPUTER MADE
YOUR OVERALL JOB EASIER?"

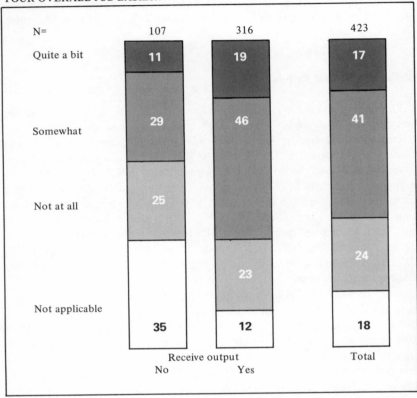

Table 6.1

OVERALL RESULTS TO THE QUESTION: AS A CONSEQUENCE OF
EDP, SKILL REQUIREMENTS IN GENERAL HAVE BEEN UPGRADED,
DOWNGRADED OR UNAFFECTED?

	Percentage responses		
Level	*Unaffected*	*Downgraded*	*Upgraded*
Clerical	31	15	54
Supervisory	30	3	67
Management	45	1	54

N=438

which might lead some observers to conclude it has been downgraded. In the customer contact areas it can be expected that in the future new functions such as selling new services will be added to the jobs which will require essentially an upgrading of skills.

The impact felt from an on-premises operation is much greater than that of one off-premises. As can be seen in Table 6.2, at every level a greater percentage of the on-premises respondents indicated that jobs had been upgraded. In the same table one can see that the chief executive officers are at the extreme positive end of the continuum on this item, and the bookkeeping officers are at the lower extreme. As for the chief executives, we think they are looking the world through slightly rose-colored glasses on this matter; however, it is probably better for them to err in the positive direction than the negative. In fairness to the bookkeeping officers, they are not as negative as the responses in Table 6.2 might imply. In fact, only 12 per cent of them felt that clerical jobs had been downgraded, as compared to 14 per cent of the total sample. A greater percentage of those in the bookkeeping department felt that there had been less absolute change at all three levels than did any of the other functional groups. The strong feeling among branch managers that skill requirements have been upgraded can be explained by the removal of the bookkeeping tasks causing the most work pressure in the branch. Their removal allows the employees to spend more time in customer contact work.

Table 6.2

PER CENT OF RESPONDENTS WHO FELT THAT CLERICAL, SUPERVISORY AND MANAGEMENT SKILLS HAVE BEEN UPGRADED BY TYPE OF EDP AND BY FUNCTIONAL AREA.

	N	Clerical	Supervisory	Management
Type of EDP				
On-premises	186	57	69	55
Off-premises	252	47	60	48
Function				
Chief exec.	35	63	77	57
Branch	27	59	74	56
Comp. oper.	28	54	64	50
Floor oper.	84	49	66	55
Loans	133	49	61	47
Bkkpg.	26	31	54	46
Total	438	51	64	51

As one would expect from earlier data on age differences, a greater percentage of the youngest age groups (59 per cent of those 30 years and under) felt that automation had upgraded management jobs than did the percentage expressing the same view in the oldest age bracket (43 per cent of those 59 years and over). To some extent, these responses may be regarded as projections of what the respondents want to happen; however, they probably also reflect fairly accurately what is actually happening to the individuals expressing the attitudes. In other words, if you do not think the computer can upgrade your job, there is a good chance it will not and vice versa.

The attitudes toward upgrading of skill requirements, especially at the managerial level, show a close relationship to the attitudes toward the intrinsic rewards of the job. For example, 63 per cent of all respondents felt EDP had made management jobs more interesting and 55 per cent said management jobs have become more challenging. In terms of job satisfaction, 44 per cent felt it had increased, while only 5 per cent felt that it had decreased, with the remaining persons feeling no change. These data refute, at this point in time, the notion that computers will dehumanize management jobs, i.e., make them dull and uninteresting. On the contrary, it is doing just the opposite and the trend can be expected to continue.

In order to maintain the level of interest in the job and be able to fulfill the new job requirements dictated by the arrival of the computer, specific skill requirements need to be acquired by banking employees. A relatively high per cent of all respondents felt the need for computer-related skills or knowledge. Managers who have had experience with their own computing system indicate a greater recognition of the need for a whole series of skills than do managers from banks using outside computer servicing. (See Table 6.3.) People from on-premises situations are likely to have a better understanding of the meaning and significance of computer-related skills, since their exposure to computer personnel is somewhat greater than those with an off-premises service.

It is interesting that both of the above groups made a sharp distinction between analytical qualities and a mathematical quantitative orientation. Both saw the former, but not the latter, as highly desirable. We can only assume that they were interpreting mathematical and quantitative in the *pure* sense and not in the sense that it is used in today's business schools.

Responses to this question by age are indicative of the value attachments of the age group. For example, in the under 31 years category the greatest per cent (69) choosing any needed quality was for *decision-making*. Only 36 per cent of the group indicated an increased need for a college education and only 29 per cent for a mathematical-quantitative orientation. This age group apparently sees decision-making as the number one glamour function of management, without really having a clear understanding of what is involved in the process. Looking at the other end of the continuum, a high per cent

(71) of the over 59 group indicated an increased need for customer contact orientation, again reflecting their own bias regarding what is ultimately important in the organization.

Table 6.3

PER CENT OF RESPONDENTS INDICATING A NEED FOR
SPECIFIC QUALITIES AS A FUNCTION OF TYPE OF EDP ARRANGEMENT.*

| Qualities needed | Type of EDP | | |
	On-premises (N=186)	Off-premises (N=252)	Total (N=438)
Computer orientation	69	56	62
Mathematicians and quantitative orientation	32	27	29
Marketing orientation	50	38	43
Customer contact	64	57	60
Decision-making skills	62	61	61
College education	47	37	42
Accounting knowledge	61	46	55
Analytical qualities	72	62	66

*Respondents were asked to choose as many areas as they felt necessary.

6.2 The Special Role of Computer Personnel

Every organization that uses computers in a significant way is faced with a man-sized problem which is not often anticipated by management, namely, how to integrate effectively the people who "make the computer go." We are referring to everyone working directly with the computer, from machine operators to managers who are responsible for coordinating the EDP activities in the bank. Regardless of whether the EDP man originally started in banking or in the computer field, he is rarely considered a banker by his fellow workers. His main responsibility is defined as computer work and handling of operations. Several of the EDP officers indicated in interviews that they did not like this trend, but most of them were realistic about its existence and felt they could do little to change it.

Computer personnel, in order to perform their jobs effectively, have to establish good relationships with other officers in the bank. At the same time, several of them, when interviewed, expressed considerable frustration in not getting the kind of cooperation they expected. There are several reasons why such lack of cooperation and frustration develops.

The "newcomer" effect. Several studies suggest that part of the influence of the EDP staff may be due to the fact that they are strangers to the organization and their limitations are not yet known (Ex, 1960). Their technical competence in an area unfamiliar to the rest of the organization may allow them a certain degree of influence, but over time this "will not suffice as a means of control without the arts of persuasion and inducement." (Martin and Sims, 1956.) In other words, a computer expert can tell someone he must keypunch input for the computer a certain way without fear of being questioned or contradicted. But when a computer expert suggests to a manager a more logical way to analyze and use data that were analyzed in a different way before, his authority for such a suggestion may well be challenged or the suggestion ignored.

Suspicion of the computer as change achiever. In the early days of the computer considerable credit was given to the capabilities of EDP. This trend is slowly changing, and while managers might still have some fear of the computer's impact, they are more inclined to judge it by actual rather than promised results. In other words, in the past, expectations of the computer were built up to such a point that now managers are requiring evidence of performance. In a study of the attitudes a task-oriented group had toward a computer as one of the members, it was reported that the computer's decisions were evaluated more critically than those of the rest of the group (Haines et. al, 1962).

Salary differential and job mobility. Computer personnel are in great demand in all industries, and consequently, their salary level has been somewhat inflated in recent years. In addition, the great demand has created a considerable job mobility among EDP personnel, who frequently move from one organization to another with the promise of improved compensation or more challenging jobs. This has created a certain degree of suspicion toward the EDP personnel so that their long-term loyalty to the organization is questioned.

Ambiguity of authority to change. The authority to introduce significant organizational change usually lies with top management and is not a prerogative which it shares freely. The introduction of a computer group often represents an exception to this rule. EDP personnel differ from other staff functions in that they are given virtually complete control of all phases in the conversion from manual to automated systems. In most cases they study the need for change, plan it, execute the conversion, and control and supervise the EDP system once it is operational. At the same time, the relationship between the EDP departments and other departments is tenuous because it is horizontal, not vertical. While EDP managers can say, "Top management wants this conversion," they usually cannot claim, "Top management wants it done in this specific way." This leaves them with little *hierarchical* authority to introduce specific changes. They usually resolve this hierarchical ambiguity by asserting their *expert* authority, which is difficult for the average manager who lacks computer knowledge to challenge.

Gaps in communication between EDP people and the remaining staff. The need for horizontal interaction is often intensified by difficulties in communication due to the fact that other managers do not understand what EDP is and should be doing. At the same time, managers in other departments complain that the EDP people do not understand enough about what they, the managers, need.

There is usually a very obvious communication problem which can only be alleviated by a great deal of mutual effort. In order to work effectively together, both the EDP personnel and the traditional managers must extend themselves, especially at the early stages of an automation program, to obtain at least a minimum understanding of the problems and working tools of each other.

Overshadowing the communication problem is the almost total dependence of the banking officers on the computer "experts" to innovate in the area of operations, because of the former group's lack of computer knowledge. Of the questionnaire respondents, 83 per cent held this attitude. This represents a very unhealthy situation when one group feels so dependent on the other with no basis of trust to offset the ambivalent feelings which are associated with dependency.

The computer people represent expertise in a very specialized area, different from the usual jobs common to banking. Yet only 39 per cent of the respondents felt that people who work directly with computers typically view the world very differently from other people in the organization, while 32 per cent disagreed with the idea. In banks using on-premises EDP the percentage of those agreeing that computer personnel view the world differently from others in the bank was somewhat higher (43 per cent). Management in those banks works more closely with the computer people, has more frequent contact with them, and as a result, is probably more accurate in its perception.

As one would expect, this attitude varies significantly as a function of the respondents' ages. It can be seen in Figure 6.2 that the percentage of those perceiving a difference between computer personnel and other banking personnel is highest for the oldest age group. One reason may be that they have the least in common with the computer group (who are generally young) and the least appreciation for their point of view.

The EDP officers themselves (68 per cent) felt most strongly that they view the world differently from other officers. Such an attitude on behalf of the computer officers can also be an important cause for disturbance in their relationships with other officers, especially if the attitude becomes known to the other officers. The notion that the computer people view the world very differently from others in the organization is also prevalent among the chief executive officers, 46 per cent of whom agreed with the statement.

FIGURE 6.2 PERCENT RESPONSE TO THE STATEMENT: PEOPLE WHO WORK DIRECTLY WITH COMPUTERS TYPICALLY VIEW THE WORLD VERY DIFFERENTLY FROM OTHER PEOPLE IN THE ORGANIZATION.

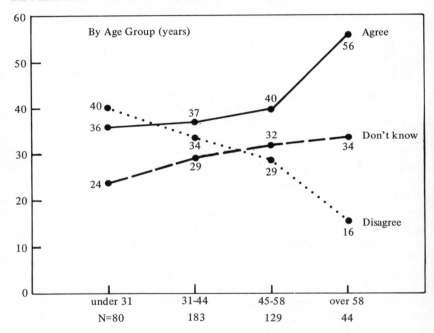

Over half of all respondents felt that whether or not EDP people view the world differently, they frequently bring a fresh point of view to banking problems and consequently represent a valuable addition to the bank. Once more, the officers in the computer functions were especially agreeable to this item (89 per cent). This again suggests the notion that one of the reasons for the existence of problems might lie in the attitude of this group that it is contributing to the bank more than other officers perceive or are willing to admit. An example of the latter are the officers in the bookkeeping functions, where only 38 per cent agreed that the computer people are a valuable addition to the bank. These are usually officers with many years of service in the bank: those whose functions have been suddenly transformed by the new EDP group.

With regard to the statement that computer personnel are frequently more intrigued with what the computer can do than with solving data processing problems in the best way possible, opinions were almost equally distributed among the three possible answers: "agree," "don't know" and "disagree." As banks gain experience with EDP, the people establish more favorable attitudes along these lines, resulting in a decrease of those saying they do not know and an increase of those disagreeing with the statement. (See Figure 6.3.) This slight but positive trend should be seen as an encouraging sign, increasing the hope for full integration of the computer personnel in the bank over time.

FIGURE 6.3 PERCENT DISAGREEING WITH THE STATEMENT: "COMPUTER PEOPLE" ARE FREQUENTLY MORE INTRIGUED WITH WHAT THE COMPUTER CAN DO THAN WITH SOLVING DATA PROCESSING PROBLEMS IN THE BEST WAY POSSIBLE.

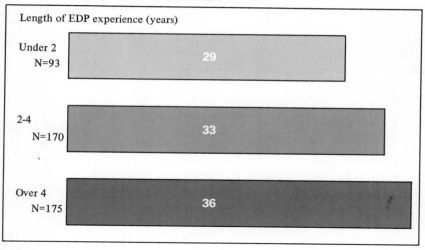

Dealing with the issue of the achievements of the computer people as measured by the effectiveness of the programs written, the accusation is often heard that computer programs are usually written by technical or staff people with little or no experience in banking which results in the expenditure of a lot of energy to produce relatively little improvement in the function being programmed. Of the total respondents, close to one-half did not agree with such an accusation, while 20 per cent said they did not know. Managers in banks using on-premises EDP are considerably more favorable than those in off-premises banks, with close to 60 per cent of the former disagreeing with the statement, compared with only 40 per cent in the off-premises arrangement. A higher percentage of officers in the off-premises banks do not have a specific opinion on the subject, probably due to their lack of contact with the programmers and EDP people.

6.3 The Computer and Personnel Advancement in the Bank

The introduction of the computer into banking is causing considerable concern on the part of many bank managers regarding their own futures in their banks. It is unfortunate that the computer has been given a great deal of credit for taking over jobs or doing away with them, but it gets very little credit for creating new jobs or making present jobs more challenging. It was only natural that most of the early applications of computers were directed toward brute force data processing and thus labor-saving projects. It is becoming more evident every day, however, that while the computer does save a lot of human effort in routine data processing, it offers unparalleled opportunities for *extending* the intelligence and creativity of managers rather than eliminating them. It may not be nearly so "obvious," however, to a manager whose views of the situation derive primarily from a limited experience with computers in his own organization.

A significant percentage of respondents expressed the feeling that the computer has caused a decrease in the number of jobs at the clerical level. (See Table 6.4.) Observations and comparisons of actual figures point out that while the absolute number of clerical workers has not decreased as one would expect, the growth in number of employees has slowed considerably, even in banks which have grown in size and volume. This represents a reduction in number needed per unit of work but not in total.

No study banks fired employees as a result of introducing the computer. Some of them gradually reduced the staff by means of normal attrition or else maintained pre-EDP levels to handle the increased volume most banks have realized in the past few years. In other words, expansion of volume and services usually absorbed those relieved from manual bookkeeping jobs. In several instances, bookkeepers were retrained as tellers, keypunch machine operators and in other jobs depending on ability and willingness. All of the study banks were quite careful in assuring employees that their jobs were secure and that no one would lose his job as a result of conversion, particularly at the clerical level. Some chose to leave anyway, but most remained.

For the supervisory and managerial levels the number of jobs remained constant or increased, the latter especially at the banks using on-premises services. Of the respondents, 87 per cent felt that supervisory jobs had either remained constant or increased in number, and 97 per cent felt this way with respect to the number of management jobs. The addition of an EDP manager

Table 6.4

EFFECT OF THE COMPUTER ON NUMBER OF JOBS

			Per cent responding		
Level of employee	Type of EDP	N	Increased	No change	Decreased
Clerical	On-premises	186	18	49	33
	Off-premises	252	15	43	41
	Total:	438	16	46	37
Supervisory	On-premises	186	54	37	10
	Off-premises	252	25	60	14
	Total:	438	37	50	12
Managerial	On-premises	186	38	60	2
	Off-premises	252	20	76	3
	Total:	438	28	69	3

or managers in banks with on-premises computers and the development of new services account for the bulk of managerial and supervisory staff additions.

With the number of jobs at the management level remaining stable or increasing somewhat, attention has turned to the changes the computer has brought with regard to present and future advancement in the bank. The main threat to the average manager is that the new computer people will monopolize the promotion routes within the organization and block the opportunities to other managers. When asked to what extent knowledge of computers affects promotion, considerably more respondents (55 per cent) felt that it would have a greater effect in the future than the number (37 per cent) who felt it has in the past. (See Table 6.5.) Chief executive officers and computer managers (57 and 54 per cent, respectively) feel more strongly than others that such knowledge has already played a role in promotion in the bank. These are the people who should know, as one group is promoted by the other for reasons of their unique value to the organization. A number of EDP managers told the interviewers that the rapid advance to their present levels was planned from the start, the actual rate being determined by the speed with which they supplemented their computer knowledge and by which new functions were automated.

Looking at Table 6.5 one can see a significant difference between on-premises and off-premises respondents, the former feeling a much greater impact in this area. This is due to the fact that in banks of equal size, there is a great deal more opportunity for a number of people to become knowledgeable about automation if the computer is on-premises. Thus their

Table 6.5

PER CENT RESPONDENTS WHO AGREE THAT PEOPLE
KNOWLEDGEABLE ABOUT COMPUTERS HAVE BEEN OR WILL BE
PROMOTED FASTER THAN OTHERS IN THE ORGANIZATION.

Type of EDP	N	Have been in the past	Will be in the future
On-premises	186	47	58
Off-premises	252	29	42
Function			
Branch manager	27	37	59
Chief executive officer	35	57	77
Computer operations	28	54	71
Floor operations	84	44	50
Bookkeeping	26	35	62
Loan officers	133	28	51
Total	438	37	55

combined knowledge of banking and automation enhances their value to the bank.

When asked about the future impact of the computer on their personal opportunities for advancement in the bank, only 27 per cent of all respondents felt that it would improve their chances, but 56 per cent of those under 31 expressed this view. (See Table 6.6.) It is understandable that a very low percentage of the older age groups feel the computer will affect their personal chances for advancement. For the most part, they are already in the upper levels of the organization and feel that they are "beyond" the computer era.

The fact that such a high per cent (93) of the computer managers feel that automation will enhance their opportunities for advancement may have a negative implication for banks. It is understandable for those who success-fully achieved automation in the bank to expect to move up in the structure, but it may also indicate a disproportionate amount of personal investment in the automation program at the expense of other phases of banking. In other words, if a computer manager is to be a full-fledged member of the banking fraternity, he should perceive other avenues of advancement to a greater extent than this response would imply. At the same time, computer officers may be building high expectations, which may lead to considerable frustration if they do not materialize fully.

It is interesting to note that despite the fact that the bookkeeping department is the one area where the computer has literally taken over jobs,

Table 6.6

PER CENT RESPONSES TO THE QUESTION:
"HOW DO YOU FEEL THE COMPUTER WILL AFFECT YOUR
PERSONAL OPPORTUNITIES FOR ADVANCEMENT IN THE BANK?"

Age	N	Will have no effect	Will improve opportunities for advancement
Under 31	80	43	57
31 to 44	183	68	32
45 to 58	129	85	14
Over 58	44	96	3
Function			
Branch manager	27	70	22
Computer operations	28	7	93
Floor operations	84	75	25
Bookkeeping	26	61	39
Loan officers	133	82	17
Total	438	70	27

39 per cent of the bookkeeping managers still perceive the computer as improving their own opportunities for advancement. This can be explained by the traditional saying, "If you can't beat 'em, join 'em." Many have in fact done just that, by becoming more computer-oriented and establishing themselves as "go-betweens" for the computer people and the remaining employees, especially in off-premises arrangements.

Only 17 per cent of the loan officers thought the computer would help their chances for advancement. It could help them without question—if they would let it—by making better use of the output and new decision-making techniques. There are still a fair number of loan officers who insist that the old ledger card was superior to the reports they get from the computer and thus maintain that the computer inhibits their function. If they ever take a long look at what is possible on the computer in this area, at least some of them would likely concede that the long-run advantages of automating this area just might outweigh the disadvantages.

6.4 Summary

While actual structure changes in the organization are slow in developing, bankers are quick to develop specific attitudes and perceptions of the impact

EDP has had on their present and future jobs, even if the impact has been minor so far. There is a prevailing attitude among bank managers that skills have generally been upgraded at all levels and especially at the supervisory level as a result of the introduction of EDP. There is also a fairly high degree of recognition of the increased need for computer-related skills and knowledge in banking.

Until the new skills are acquired there will exist some tension between the computer managers and other members of the work force in the bank. Such tension is more likely to exist when "outsiders" are brought in to manage the EDP operations. The tension is often a result of the way the computer and its staff are introduced into the bank and the general adverse reaction most people have to a forced change. At the same time it seems to be, in part at least, the fault of the computer personnel who consider themselves different from others in the bank and consequently help create a gap in communication between themselves and other personnel. It can be expected that with the increase in experience with EDP some of the mystery surrounding EDP will diminish and the attitude of bank officers toward computer people will become more positive.

Top management will have to pay increasing attention in order to reduce tension and to keep its employees satisfied in the area of advancement in the organization. Bank managers believe the computer will enhance the advancement opportunities of those with knowledge in the area of EDP. The trend has already started, particularly in banks using on-premises computers, and should accelerate in the next few years as bankers begin to realize the value of such knowledge.

Chapter 7

Training

for the Computer Era

The problem of training in today's banks represents a qualitatively and quantitatively different kind of problem than it did for the banker of 20 years ago. There are at least four reasons why this is so (Vaughan and Porat, 1968). First, the changes in the banking industry over the last two decades have created new and different skill requirements. Some of these new skills can be learned on the job, but others, requiring specialized knowledge, can be learned effectively only in off-the-job training courses. Second, the number of new employees who come into banking annually continues to be high, relative to other industries. Thus, the sheer numbers who need training suggest the need for an organized program for the entire bank rather than the haphazard approach of the past. Third, the costs associated with hiring, developing and holding competent employees represent a sizeable investment which is increasing yearly. In order to compete successfully with other industries for the best talent, banks will be forced to invest more in human development. Finally, many banks—especially those below $50 million in deposits—have a real void below the highest level of management. A common pattern in the small bank is a situation where one or two senior officers make all the major decisions and the junior officers never even participate in the process. If management succession is to be orderly and not disruptive, this pattern must be modified.

7.1 On-the-Job Training

One consequence of the changes in the industry described above is that on-the-job training is not as effective in developing employees as it was in the past. It used to be possible to rotate a new employee through a number of jobs and, with proper guidance, give him a very satisfactory grasp of banking. The aspiring manager learned his job in large part through "data experience." That is, a manager used to acquire a certain "feel" for decison-making as a consequence of personally handling or processing much of the relevant data or information pertaining to the decision.

It is difficult to assess the importance of day-to-day "data experience" in general, but due to the rapid shifts in the banking industry, one can see how it can have a restricting effect on some managers. For example, managers often report difficulties in utilizing information when, as a result of automation, data is handled by the computer and presented in new forms. Previously, they were accustomed to being intimately involved in data processing, and based their decisions on their "data experience." Now the same decisions have to be made on the basis of information compiled by others and presented in a new format, usually a summary report. Obviously, the nature of the summary report is very critical. It may well present the data in such a way that decision-making is made much easier and, one would hope, result in better decisions. On the other hand, it may do just the opposite—confuse the users.

The real benefit from experiencing the data firsthand would vary according to the relevance of the "data experience" to the final decision to be made. One can see, for example, how a loan officer would be able to deal more effectively in terms of personal service with individual customers when he is personally familiar with their transactions and involved in collecting and assessing the relevant information. This relative advantage must be weighed, however, against the worth of freeing the loan officer from daily involvement in data processing and permitting him to use that time in other areas which also influence his effectiveness as a loan officer. At any rate, many of tomorrow's managers will not have the previously described advantage, however great it may be. Instead, they will have to rely on the computer. They will need different kinds of skills and competencies from those of their predecessors and they will probably have to learn these in very different ways. They will still learn by making decisions, but the decisions will be based on redefined "data experience" and require additional knowledge of EDP, analytical techniques of decision-making, and other related areas.

Bankers, themselves, share this viewpoint. In the current study, 365 respondents (84.9 per cent) agreed that bank management jobs of the future will require a much greater understanding of the analytic techniques of decision-making, 6.7 per cent disagreed and 8.4 per cent said they did not know. These techniques will probably have to be learned in formal training programs. We are not arguing that on-the-job training has no value in banking today. We are suggesting that it is necessary to supplement it with off-the-job educational experiences. *The need for specialists in today's banks often supersedes the need for the all-around banker.* Or, to put it another way, in many banks the data processing operations are completely separate from the floor function being supported. Thus a mortgage loan officer may be very effective without being involved in the operations end of loan accounting.

7.2 Off-the-Job Training

The day-to-day immersion in a job often prevents the kinds of changes in behavior desired from training programs. Therefore, there is a need to supplement or substitute on-the-job training with off-the-job programs. Off-the-job training has some distinct advantages. First, it can provide training in specialized skills required in different areas of banking. Courses offered by professional associations cover such diverse areas as auditing, accounting, operations, personnel, data processing, taxes and market research. Other programs covering specific areas in detail or providing general training at beginner or advanced levels are offered by universities and other educational institutions. The organizations offering the training programs are usually better equipped and staffed for this purpose than are the individual banks, especially the small ones. Such programs expose the students to professional resource people and materials (faculty members, fellow bankers and books) and hopefully challenge him to maximize the opportunity to develop himself.

A second advantage of off-the-job training programs is found in the opportunity to concentrate on a particular area of study free from interruptions and other responsibilities. Thus, it is possible to learn skills more quickly and effectively and then put them to use back on the job. A third advantage is that the banker is given the opportunity of interacting with others in his profession. This exchange of experience and information in an organized forum can be a significant learning experience for the participants and can form the basis of fruitful professional relationships.

There are also some disadvantages to off-the-job training which should be mentioned. The primary one is that the persons participating in such programs are often away from the bank during banking hours, forcing others to fill in for them. Another disadvantage is the cost involved in sending people to off-premises programs. The authors recognize that both factors can put some burden on the bank, especially the smaller ones, but believe that in the long run, the pay-off will justify the expenditure. In many cases, the major objections to sending people to courses reflect top management's biases against the need for such courses, biases which are considerably influenced by the traditional independence of the banker. The problem for top management, then, should not be whether to use off-premises training, but rather to decide what mix of on-the-job and off-the-job training will be most effective.

There will always be a temptation to resort exclusively to the "tried and true" method of on-the-job training or "learning while doing," which has worked for so long in the past. In smaller banks especially, some managers will continue to feel that they cannot afford the luxury of off-the-job training. They think on-the-job training is better for them because the trainee is doing necessary work or because he is "paying his way" while learning. The truth of this argument depends upon the time required for training and the relative cost of training as measured by the trainee's effectiveness on the job. We observed some banks which were very proud of the fact that their employees had taught themselves to program a computer and had handled the entire process of automation without outside help. This is admirable, but in our opinion, they could have reached their present state of development in much less time and with fewer costly errors, if their people had had the appropriate training by competent professionals.

7.3 Planned Training Program

It is not possible to arrive at a prescriptive program that will meet the educational needs of all banks, or even all banks of a given size or geographic area. Each bank must perform a careful analysis of its particular circumstances in order to determine its training needs. Three kinds of analyses are appropriate: (1) An organization analysis should be performed on the whole bank—its objectives, its resources, the allocation of these resources in meeting its objectives, and the total socio-economic-technological environment within which the bank operates. Such an analysis establishes the content of the training program in terms of broad content areas and thus sets the tone or philosophy of training for the entire organization. (See Chapter 3.) (2) Job analyses should be performed on all jobs. This involves a careful study of specific jobs within the organization to further define the content of training. (3) Finally, a manpower analysis should be made of all the present employees to determine whether performance is substandard and training is needed and whether current employees can profit from training.

Based on the information accumulated in the above analysis, top management can develop a training program that will outline the objectives and utilize the available on- and off-the-job training possibilities. Such a program should become an integral part of employee development and provide the depth for effective management succession.

Training needs and methods are changing in all areas of work in the bank, but the need for training is especially high in those areas which did not exist in the past or have changed drastically. The computer has probably caused the most significant changes with respect to training. There is a growing need for computer specialists in banks, such as programmers and operators, but also for a host of other specialists. As a direct offshoot of large-scale computer operations and the vast quantities of information generated, specialists in areas such as operations research, market analysis and cost accounting are becoming very much in demand by banks. Specialists in those areas often have no prior experience in banking and must acquire a knowledge of banking in order to perform their jobs effectively.

At the same time, aspiring bankers must learn something of EDP for effective job performance in addition to in-depth training in the area of their specialty. Their EDP education need not be of a detailed technical nature but instead may take the form of learning about computer operations and capabilities in general. Managers require a different level of training, perhaps in more abstract terms, than do clerical employees who handle more of the nuts and bolts of the input-output process. Both in the case of the computer expert and the banking employee, part of his training is perhaps most effectively done on-the-job, while more general training in concepts of banking and EDP may be best accomplished by attending off-the-job courses, seminars and workshops.

7.4 Management Attitudes Towards Training

In order to assess management attitudes towards these issues, two questions were asked: (1) What types of training are required for which people in order that they may perform their jobs more effectively? and (2) What methods are most appropriate for each type of training and for each group of trainees? Each question will be discussed in turn.

7.4.1 Training Needed for the Individual and for Various Employee Levels

One general result worth noting is that with the exception of preparing computer input, more managers felt that "management" as a group has greater need for the various types of training than each has individually. (See Table 7.1.) In other words, they were quite consistent in saying that "what is good for my fellow managers is not necessarily good for me." It also reflects a commonly held attitude of a large number of managers in all industries, to the effect that " 'others' need training more than I do."

Table 7.1

EXPRESSED TRAINING NEEDS FOR ONESELF AND VARIOUS
EMPLOYEE LEVELS, IN PER CENT

	Per cent of total respondents indicating useful to essential training for:			
Training needed	*Self*	*Clerical*	*Supervisory*	*Management*
Basic programming	25	16	36	27
Reading and interpreting output	54	36	62	61
Preparing computer input	23	52	51	21
Statistical analysis and mathema- tical tools	38	6	35	48
Capabilities of the computer	48	11	53	58
Accounting principles	40	16	47	47
Information retrieval and analysis	41	12	45	50
Model construction and utilization	19	5	24	27

N=438

Looking at all the training needs listed in Table 7.1, it can be seen that the one felt to be most important across all groups is reading and interpreting computer output. This corroborates the feeling expressed earlier that reports generated by the computer are not being used in an optimally effective way.

Second in importance for the two top levels is training in the capabilities of the computer. If anyone in the bank has had either of these kinds of training, it is usually the president and/or operations officer who is charged with the responsibility of determining available EDP arrangements and recommending which to use. Others in the bank may have received a half-day presentation, by the computer manufacturer or representative from the outside service center, on what reports look like. These two types of training are interdependent, since in order to effectively plan modifications in existing reports and to request new ones, the manager should know how to interpret the existing reports as well as have a general understanding of what the computer can and cannot do.

Managers feel the least need to get training for themselves in preparing computer input and in model construction and utilization. Our own feeling is that very few managers in the study banks have a clear understanding of how models are constructed, how they are used in problem solving and what is involved in maintaining or updating models. Widespread activity in this area, i.e., use of models, is probably several years away in most small banks. When it does come about, however, managers will be involved in preparing input to the computer, but it will be a very different kind of input from that which goes into the computer today. In the future, managers will be manipulating the parameters of models they helped to construct in order to test the probable effects of alternate decisions. More will be said about this later in the chapter.

The training needs of the clerical staff, from management's point of view, are primarily in preparing computer input, with somewhat less need for reading and interpreting computer output. All other types of training were seen as generally not relevant to this group. In our opinion, these results represent a relatively unenlightened point of view. Clerical personnel play a very critical support role in the automation program, and it is important for them to be adequately aware of the capabilities of EDP and its role in the organization. Otherwise, they will continue to be a weak link in the system, capable of performing some well-defined, repetitive functions but unable to contribute to organizational or their own personal growth.

As one might expect, a high per cent (71) of EDP managers felt a significant need for training in information retrieval and analysis. This is, of course, the key to the development of a Central Information File or to an automated Management Information System (MIS). It may be that one could build an effective, automated MIS in a small bank a lot easier than in a large one, since the problems are much less complex and certainly exist on a smaller scale. Nevertheless, we found no significant progress in this direction in our study.

7.4.2 General Training Considerations

A question in the minds of many managers interviewed in the current study is whether to teach bankers computer science or hire computer experts and teach them banking. When asked this question, 41 per cent of the managers felt it was easier to teach "computer people" the banking industry, 41 per cent felt just the reverse and 17 per cent said they did not know. (See Table 7.2.)

The tendency to overestimate the uniqueness of one's own profession is quite evident in these data. Of the computer managers, 85 per cent felt it was easier to teach "computer people" banking than vice versa, whereas 52 per cent of the "dyed-in-the-wool" bankers (branch managers and chief executives) expressed the opposite point of view. As indicated earlier, placing a banker in charge of the computer operation and training him in computer technology would probably serve to reduce internal conflict and resistance to the automation program. This is due mainly to the fact that any non-banker coming into the bank, no matter how knowledgeable he is about banking, must go through some initiation before becoming an accepted member of the banking fraternity. Nevertheless, it is possible and desirable for persons trained in either of the two professions to become competent in the other;

and in our opinion, the need for cross-education is much greater than is recognized.

Table 7.2

PER CENT RESPONDING TO THE STATEMENT:
"IT IS EASIER TO GIVE 'COMPUTER PEOPLE' AN UNDERSTANDING OF
THE BANKING INDUSTRY THAN TO GIVE 'BANKING PEOPLE'
AN UNDERSTANDING OF THE COMPUTER."

Function	N	Disagree	Don't know	Agree
Branch manager	27	52	33	15
Chief executive officer	35	51	9	40
Computer operations	28	11	34	86
Floor operations	84	43	18	38
Bookkeeping managers	26	35	13	51
Loan officers	133	47	21	32
Total	438	41	17	41

7.4.3 Techniques Deemed Most Appropriate for Computer-Related Training

The technique judged most effective for acquiring EDP training was periodic lectures or seminars in the bank. (See Table 7.3.) The second most favored technique was periodic visits to the computer center. This is telling evidence that in the main, managers attach relatively little importance to training and have little real understanding about what is involved in training. They talk a lot about training, but they do precious little about it. Training can wait—and it usually does as other pressing day-to-day problems crowd it out. Or if it must be done, then according to these attitudes, it can be done in little bits and pieces or on the employee's own time (50 per cent indicated that evening courses would be appropriate). This is admittedly drawing a hard line here, since 69 per cent also said that five- to ten-day off-the-job courses were appropriate, but the fact still remains that there is far too little investment in the bank's greatest resource—people.

Almost any orientation, training or exposure to a computer is better than none at all; however, sporadic lectures or tours through a computer facility are probably the least effective means of educating people about automation. Computer manufacturers offer some short-term orientation courses which are helpful; yet, they are understandably designed to sell their companies' computers, so they leave something to be desired in terms of their generality and attention given to practical problems.

There are many different views as to the form that computer orientation training should take for people who will be working with computer output and who need to understand something about the way the computer handles data, but who probably will never do any major programming themselves. At one extreme is the view that one must become a fairly proficient programmer and learn a good deal about the systems approach to organizational problems in order to acquire the necessary understanding. At the other extreme is the point of view that in one- or two-day orientation programs covering basic computer components and auxiliary equipment, along with some material about the capabilities of computers, the job can be accomplished. The best answer lies somewhere in between and is dependent upon the trainees in question. It is extremely difficult for most people to conceptualize how a computer program actually operates without going through the learning process of writing a few short programs themselves. This can, however, be accomplished in 3 or 4 days of intensive study. One can also learn a great deal about systems concepts and computer capabilities in two or three days.

Such intensive courses will not make proficient programmers or systems analysts of the participants. They can serve, however, to remove the aura of mystery from the computer and as a base for further learning.

Table 7.3

APPROPRIATENESS OF VARIOUS TRAINING TECHNIQUES
FOR COMPUTER OR EDP TRAINING, IN PER CENT

	Appropriate	Not appropriate	Don't know
Periodic visits to computer center	80	17	3
Periodic lectures or seminars in the bank	86	9	5
Short-term courses (5 to 10 days) in a computer center or school	69	24	7
Long-term, detailed courses (1 month) away from the bank	19	72	9
An evening course once or twice a week	50	42	8
State or national automation conventions	34	53	13

N=330

7.5 Training in Model Construction and Utilization

In the long run, the most effective use of the computer will be in the application of sophisticated management science techniques which are based in the main on the concept of modeling. In general terms, a model is any representation of a prototype object or system. A model permits simulated behavior of the prototype in at least some ways which indicate how the prototype would behave under different conditions. All managers use models of one sort or another in planning, evaluating, and decision-making. In fact it is probably fair to say that a manager is only as effective as his models of the business enterprise.

The computer makes possible the construction and application of very powerful and sophisticated models, but because men must build the models, the possible outcomes will be a direct function of the combined knowledge and skill applied in the construction. Moreover, modeling on a computer involves more than simply transferring human thinking and decision-making into a machine language and computer output. Perhaps the computer's main value is that it literally forces one to be painfully explicit and exact when defining relationships in a model.

Continuous modification and updating of a model are necessary at all levels of the organization in today's environment but it is especially true in the upper levels of an organization. A company cannot be rigidly designed, like a machine, around a fixed goal. Over time a smaller and smaller portion of decisions can be programmed for future use, and the highest activity of management becomes a continuous process of decision-making about the very nature of the business itself.

Not just a few, but a great many managers will be involved in this process of model building and utilization, and it will require not only their know-how and creativity but some additional education. In their enthusiasm and optimism for the potential of the computer many proponents tended to overlook or minimize the time and cost in man-hours needed in the development of computer applications. A complex model can require many months and even years to develop, and once it has been developed, it must be maintained, i.e., updated if it is to continue to reflect reality. This process will require more rather than fewer managers in the future.

With a sophisticated model, one will be able to ask questions like: "What would happen if we relocate our branch next to the office of competitor A rather than near competitor B's office?" or "What would happen if we raised the interest charges ¼ per cent and at the same time extended the maximum time allowed for the payment of installment loans?" One will be able to ask these and many more questions but the answers one gets will only be as good as the models he has built.

Management must be intimately involved in the whole process of model construction if it is to be satisfied with the ultimate outcome and hence it must learn something about the tools and techniques as well as the process involved in sophisticated modeling. This will include two major aspects: the construction of models and their utilization. The manager of the future will not spend all or most of his time constructing models. The main job of model construction will fall on the shoulders of the staff people—the operations research analysts, the systems people, etc. However, the manager must supervise and direct his staff and participate in the total activity by contributing his own knowledge to the process.

Many of today's managers who have access to systems or operations research staffs find themselves in a position where they are directed, or even manipulated, by the technical staff rather than directing it. The computer and systems people learn to use the management language to convince management that what they are proposing is the correct thing, but the manager does not have the education and training to question the model. We have observed several cases where management was presented proposals to operate in a certain way, using given models, and told it was the best way, or even the only right way, to accomplish the job. The systems people presenting the models insisted they had the best knowledge available, and when managers raised questions the systems people retreated to technical terms and language which the manager could not understand or judge. Here is where communication breaks down between the manager and the computer or systems people. In many instances this communication gap is used to the benefit of the computer people and not always to the best utilization of team efforts for the organization. This leads us to one of the main goals in management education for modeling. The manager should be trained to analyze a model presented to him by his staff.

Like a good researcher, as the first step in testing the model's validity the manager needs to be able to ask the right questions of it and the staff who constructed it. He also needs to understand the limitations of modeling and the computing equipment which will be used to execute the model so that he can suggest modifications and improvements which are within the limits of reason and consequently do not frustrate his technical staff.

The managerial environment of the future will be one of tremendous excitement and challenge. Managers at all levels of the organization will have better information as well as more sophisticated tools of decision-making at their disposal, but the decisions they will be called upon to make will also have increased in complexity. There is no danger of managerial jobs becoming dull and routine. What is needed, however, is the development of educational programs which will prepare managers to cope with the organizational world of the future, programs that will allow the manager to become the leader of a team rather than a follower who must depend upon his technical staff. Like the development of sophisticated computer applications, the development of adequate educational programs will be a costly undertaking requiring a great deal of research and experimentation. If the past is any predictor of the future, many organizations will be unwilling to commit the necessary money and man-hours to accomplish the task, but the consequences are likely to be far more serious than in the past.

Chapter 8

Maintaining
and Refining an Automation Program

As we indicated in previous chapters, all of the study banks are still in what we would term the data processing phase of automation. That is, they have not gone beyond the very lowest level of computer applications, namely, the straightforward conversion of a manual system to an automated one. The most exciting phase of the application of management science techniques via the computer lies ahead of them.

Just how far ahead this next phase is for the small to medium-sized bank is difficult to estimate. The investment in research which is required to maintain a full blown management science program is probably prohibitive for the small to medium-sized bank. Their participation then, in this phase of automation, will depend to a great extent on other sources making available applications which have been tested and found to be effective. At least five such sources include: large banks which can afford management science programs, professional banking associations such as the ABA and BAI, consulting firms, computer manufacturers and computer software companies, and universities (especially schools of business with strong management science programs).[1]

---

[1] For an excellent summary of the current status and future of management science in banking, see Frederick Hammer's 1967 series in *Banker's Monthly Magazine.*

Before a bank even considers the use of management science techniques, however, it should have its basic data processing in order. At present many banks are in a period of consolidation in this regard. That is, after rushing head-long into an automation program without adequate study of their own needs and the alternatives available to them, they are now taking a hard look at their progress and realizing in many instances that their earlier decisions were not the most appropriate ones for the bank. In some cases a few minor adjustments may serve to put the automation program on the right track; in others, a change to a completely different form of automation will be required. At any rate, a substantial number of banks that have already launched automation programs will have a considerable amount of housecleaning to do before they can make effective use of management science techniques.

There is some irony in the way managers in banks as well as other industries view change with regard to time perspective. On the one hand, there is a general reluctance to give up the tried and true methods of operating so that specific changes in this regard are slowed down. On the other hand, automation in the abstract is a very attractive concept to managers and most of them want their organizations to be automated as of "yesterday." One of the most useful conclusions which can be drawn from this and other studies of automation is that a realistic time perspective is critical to the success of the program.

8.1 The Right Time Perspective

Developing an effective automation program is a long-term proposition. There are at least two primary reasons it is a task that cannot be achieved quickly. First, there is no such thing as a final organizational system. Further research will continue to improve techniques of management science and systems design so that there will always be reason to change and modify systems. Second, a system which is apparently optimal today can be outdated tomorrow because of the dynamic environment in which organizations exist. At the same time, it would be unusual for an entire system to become outmoded overnight. The more likely case is that some aspects of the total system will be under constant revision in order to reflect changes in the environment. It is vital that top management recognize the continuous nature of this process and be willing to commit the necessary human and financial resources to it. Otherwise, management, as well as the computer personnel, will be in for a long series of frustrations.

There is a bright side to this picture. One can reasonably expect a fairly steady stream of improvements as the program develops. The progress will not always be smooth, as there will be some "breakthroughs" and some slow periods, but the point is, a bank does not have to wait three to five years to begin reaping benefits from its automation program. There is ample evidence in the current study that some benefits are realized almost immediately and then continue to increase over time.

In looking at Figure 8.1 this trend becomes obvious. It is no doubt disappointing to some that the computer does not aid more in reducing costs in the early years. It is encouraging, however, to see that the number of managers who felt that it had decreased costs increased with the length of EDP experience of the bank from a low of 3 per cent with banks having less than two years experience to 23 per cent with those having over 4 years experience. (It should be remembered that these are managers' perceptions of the effect on costs—not necessarily the actual effect). While in the past many bank managers saw in the use of the computer a way to save direct operation costs, most bank managers today see as their goal maintenance of cost and prevention of increases. It is realistic, in fact, to expect an increase in cost in the short run and then a decrease over time. On a related item a slightly more favorable response was obtained. Among bank managers using computers for less than two years, 15 per cent felt that the computer had enabled them to make better use of the bank's funds, whereas 33 per cent of those in banks using computers for more than 4 years expressed this attitude.

In sum, Figure 8.1 provides a good summary from the bank managers' point of view of many of the observations which we have made in earlier chapters. First, they have viewed the computer as a solution to many of the data processing problems which constituted a considerable burden on the bank. This is the area where they put most of their computer effort and consequently realized their most immediate benefits. As can be seen in Figure 8.1, the three items on which the most improvement was reported are all related to basic data processing. The next four items in terms of perceived improvement are second order benefits in the sense that they can only be achieved when the first three show improvement. For example, in order to make possible better management control, one must improve the quality of information and the speed of operations in general.

In the second four-year period of a bank's use of computers, one could expect a continuing gradual increase in improvement of the basic data processing but an acceleration in the rate of improvement of the secondary items such as providing better service to customers and so on. Enabling better use of money and decreasing the cost of operations can be considered third order improvements in terms of our discussion. That is, as improvements in data processing enable managers to gain more effective control over their operations, they will be able to reduce costs and make better use of the bank's money. Improvements in these third order items should continue to

FIGURE 8.1 PER CENT OF RESPONDENTS INDICATING THEY HAVE OBSERVED A CONSIDERABLE IMPROVEMENT IN THE FOLLOWING AREAS AS A RESULT OF THE INTRODUCTION OF EDP IN THEIR BANK.

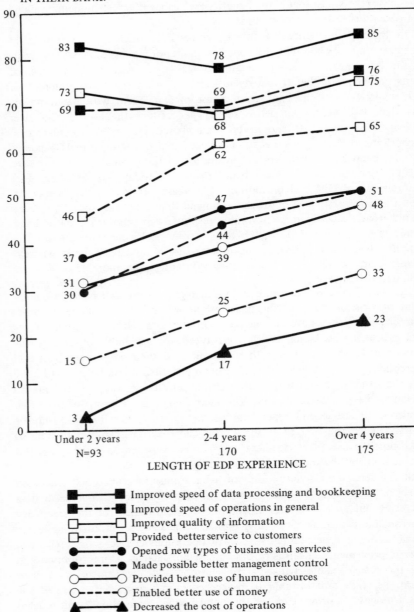

LENGTH OF EDP EXPERIENCE

■——■ Improved speed of data processing and bookkeeping
■----■ Improved speed of operations in general
□——□ Improved quality of information
□----□ Provided better service to customers
●——● Opened new types of business and services
●----● Made possible better management control
○——○ Provided better use of human resources
○----○ Enabled better use of money
▲——▲ Decreased the cost of operations

increase at a gradual rate. The introduction of management science techniques can further accelerate these improvements.

We see no reason to doubt that the use of computers in banking will continue to increase in terms of the number of banks using computers and the number of applications within specific banks. This should pose no particular threat to bank managers. It should be clear by now that computers do not take over management jobs and management responsibilities. They can, however, change management jobs and provide significant assistance to management decision-making so that managers can better meet their responsibilities to the organization. As Hammer (1967) points out, "Management science is a decision-making aid, not a decision-maker." Furthermore, it provides management with insights and information which make possible improvements in the quality of management decisions. As the banking environment becomes more complex, the relative contributions of management science techniques can be expected to become even more important.

In order for these improvements to be realized, however, bank managers must accept the fact that they themselves are an indispensable part of the management science team. As indicated in Chapter 7, this does not mean that they will have to become experts in the mathematical techniques involved. It does mean, however, that they will have to develop sufficient understanding of the applicability of the techniques so that they can make intelligent judgments as to when certain techniques are appropriate and as to when they should rely on the specialists. This will, of course, require a great deal of bank management's time. However, as the problems which it faces become steadily more complex, management will have no choice in the matter.

8.2 The Right People

We have already commented in various places on the importance of having qualified people in the EDP operation. It is necessary, however, to distinguish between computer personnel and management scientists. The management scientist is one who is trained in the techniques of quantitative approaches to problem-solving and decision-making. He is first a researcher and secondarily, a technician in specifying the precise application of the outcomes of his research. Since he uses the computer extensively in carrying out his research, most management scientists are competent in using computers. This does not mean, however, that any management scientist would make a good EDP manager for a bank. In fact, his use of computers is usually a highly specialized one and does not give him the general expertise which would be desired in a computer manager.

The manager of an EDP system, on the other hand, should have a broad-based understanding of computer equipment and computer applications. He should be familiar with existing software and should be capable of supervising the development of software for the bank. In all probability he will be familiar with some management science techniques, but his competence in this area will not compare with that of the management scientist. Most small banks will not be able to afford both computer specialists and management scientists. Their best alternative will be to hire a competent computer person who is capable of at least keeping up with the developments in management science and applying the techniques as they become available. Furthermore, the computer manager must be more than a competent technician. He must be able to talk with other bank managers on their terms and he must develop an understanding and appreciation of the problems they face. In all probability he will spend more than half of his time communicating and working with other management groups. This may seem like a rather costly use of his time, but it is a necessary one if the applications which he and his staff develop are to be understood and successfully implemented by other bank managers.

One of the ironies of this situation is the fact that the truly competent computer man is likely to be more controversial and cause more conflict in the organization than the rudderless interloper who "fakes" his way along while talking a good game. Computer work is still so new that the flash-in-the-pan interloper can look just as good in the short-run to his management as can the competent computer pioneer. What is needed is competent computer men who also have an appreciation of the issues involved in managing organizational change. In most of the study banks a critical element needed for effective change was missing. We are referring to the collaborative process. In order for planned change to be effected in an automation program, there must be a relationship established between the computer personnel and the other managers such that control and dependency are balanced and the relationship is completely open for examination and reconstruction by both parties. There must be a joint effort that involves mutual determination of goals, a free spirit of inquiry and a reliance on determinations based on data publicly shared. This poses considerable difficulty for many bank managers who are accustomed to treating the data they work with in a highly confidential manner and who are often highly resistant to change—especially that introduced by "strangers."

8.3 The Right Attitude Towards Change

It is fitting to conclude this book with a discussion of organizational change since it would be virtually impossible to introduce EDP into an organization without causing some changes in the system. As noted above, resistance to change is a very normal and predictable reaction on the part of managers in any organization. Two possible exceptions to this axiom are (1) when the present methods of operating are not effective and are close to collapse and (2) when a receptive attitude towards change has been created prior to the change itself in the organization. The question then becomes, how does one create an openness to change?

Traditionally, organizations have not been designed to facilitate change. In fact, they have been designed to achieve just the opposite of change, namely, control and stability. The typical bank is a prime example of such a traditional organization. Areas of responsibility and lines of authority are clearly specified so that all organizational activities can be closely monitored and controlled. This is, of course, important. However, some of the consequences are unfortunate and can be avoided. The traditional organization, for example, inhibits horizontal communication and causes managers to develop feelings of propriety regarding their part of the operation. When such feelings exist, the managers in question are likely to withhold information and thus delay or inhibit meaningful collaboration with other departments which might result in improvements for both.

An organization cannot "change its colors" overnight. Many organizations are more likely to avoid it as long as they possibly can and then do a mediocre job if they are forced to make some internal changes. It is possible, of course, for top management to dictate change and this does occur. What is needed, however, is the development of an attitude of openness towards change throughout the organization such that managers from different departments are able to collaborate in the recognition and definition of problems, in generating creative solutions to the problems, and finally in implementing these solutions.

There are two principal techniques for developing such an attitude both of which are appropriate for and within the means of banks of all sizes. They could, in fact, be used simultaneously. The first technique involves the use of task forces for finding a solution to problems which have general implications for the bank as a whole. A task force is composed of managers from different departments and is given responsibility for developing the solution for one or more specific problems. In most instances the task force responsibility will occupy only a portion of a manager's job. In some cases, however, a manager is relieved of his regular job for a period of time during which he works full-time on the task force assignment. This provides an opportunity for managers to get outside their own family groups and develop a better appreciation of the problems of other family groups. The length of time the task force exists will depend upon the specific nature of its assignment. When the task force has completed its assignment and is disbanded, however, the hope is that new consulting relationships and communication channels will have been established that will continue over time.

The second technique involves training managers in the management of change. There is a sizeable body of literature now available concerning planning and implementing organizational change. Many universities and consulting firms offer short and long programs on this topic. An ideal strategy for a bank would be to send selected managers to several different programs of this sort, thus maximizing the input to the organization. Combining such training with the use of cross-departmental task forces should enable a bank to maximize its responsiveness to internal as well as external stimuli to change. It is only in this kind of organizational atmosphere that the bank can hope to integrate its management team, the new management science techniques and the computer into an operational system of maximum effectiveness.

References

American Banking Association. 1966 *National Automation Survey – Projection* (unpublished survey). New York: 1966.

Anderson, A. H. (et al). *An Electronic Cash and Credit System.* New York: American Management Association, 1966.

Ankeny, Lloyd D. "Small Bank EDP Servicing," *Auditgram,* Vol. 63, No. 10 (October 1967), 10.

Dale, Edwin. *The Decision-making Process in the Commercial Use of High-Speed Computers.* (Cornell Studies in Policy and Administration) Ithaca, Cornell University Graduate School of Business and Public Administration, 1964.

Ex, J. "The Nature of the Relation between Two Persons and the Degree of Influence on Each Other," *Acta Psychologica* XVII (1960), 39-54.

Federal Deposit Insurance Corporation. *Annual Report* (1947-1967). Washington, D. C.: 1948-1968.

Haines, G. F. Heider and D. Remington. "The Computer as a Small Group Member," *Administration Science Quarterly,* VI (1962), 360-374.

Hamid, Mohammed Kahlil. "Price and Output Decision in the Computer Industry." Unpublished Ph.D. dissertation, University of Iowa, 1966.

Hammer, Frederick S. "Managing Management Science," *Bankers Monthly* (February 15, 1967), 26-32.

Judson, Arnold Sidney, *A Manager's Guide to Making Changes.* New York: John Wiley and Sons, 1966.

Mann, F. C. *The Impact of Electronic Accounting Equipment on the White Collar Worker: Summary of comments made as a panel member on "Automation in the Office" at the Society for Applied Anthropolgy Conference on Man and Automation, under the Auspices of the Institute for Social Research, University of Michigan, December 27-28, 1955.*

Martin, N. H. and J. H. Sims. "Thinking Ahead: Power Tactics," *Harvard Business Review,* Vol. 34, No. 6 (November/December, 1956), 25-29.

Mitchell, G. W. *Confrontation Within Banking: Machines vs. Bankers or Bankers vs. Machines: Speech at the National Automation Conference, American Bankers Association, at Chicago on June 6, 1966.*

Moll, Robert E. "The Design and Implementation of a Management Information System," *Bank Administration,* Vol. 64, No. 10 (October, 1968) 22-26.

Myers, Charles Andrew, ed. *The Impact of Computers on Management.* Cambridge: The M.I.T. Press, 1967.

Nadler, Paul S. "What Stunts the Growth of Demand Deposits," *Banking,* Vol. 6, No. 7, (January, 1964), 52-53.

Porat, A. M. and J. A. Vaughan. "Branch Management and Computers," *Banking,* Vol. 60, No. 3 (September, 1967), 121-124.

Rico, Leonard. *The Advance Against Paperwork: Systems, Computers and Personnel.* Ann Arbor: University of Michigan, Graduate School of Business Administration, Bureau of Industrial Relations, 1967.

Robinson, R. I. *The Management of Bank Funds* (2nd ed.) New York: McGraw Hill Book Co., Inc., 1962.

Sanders, D. H. *Introducing Computers to Small Business.* Park Ridge, Illinois: Data Processing Management Association, 1966.

U. S. Department of Commerce, Office of Business Economics. *Business Statistics: The Biennial Supplement to the Survey of Current Business* (16th ed.). Washington, D. C.: 1967. pp. 65-82.

Vaughan, J. A. and A. M. Porat. "Managerial Reaction to Computers," *Banking,* Vol. 59, No. 10 (April, 1967), 119-122.

Vaughan, J. A. and A. M. Porat. "Management Education in the Computer Age," *Training and Development Journal,* Vol. 22, No. 3 (March, 1968), 58-65.

Wiener, Rose. "Changing Manpower Requirements in Banking," *Monthly Labor Review,* Vol. 85, No. 9 (September, 1962), 989-995.

Yavitz, B. *Automation in Commercial Banking: Its Process and Impact.* New York: The Free Press, 1967.

Sample Description: Selected Data Classified
by Type of EDP Arrangement (in Per cent)

A.	Economic variables	*Total*	*On-premises*	*Off-premises*	*No EDP*
	Number of banks	57	18	31	8
	1. *Size of deposits*				
	Under $25 million	61%	33%	74%	75%
	Over $25 million	39	67	26	25
	2. *Ratio of demand deposits to total deposits*				
	Under 45 per cent	53	44	58	50
	45-55 per cent	26	28	29	12
	Over 55 per cent	21	28	13	38
	3. *Ratio of growth of deposits 1964-66*				
	Under 9 per cent	14	22	13	0
	10-29 per cent	49	61	39	62
	30-49 per cent	25	17	26	38
	50 per cent or more	12	0	23	0

13

	Total	On-premises	Off-premises	No EDP
4. *Net income before tax per $100 of assets (1966)*				
Under 60¢	30	22	42	0
60-79¢	49	50	42	75
Over 80¢	21	28	16	25
5. *Branches*				
No branches	42	40	52	12
At least 1 branch	58	60	48	88
B. EDP variables				
Number of banks	49	18	31	N/A
1. *Length of EDP experience*				
Under 2 years	18%	17%	19%	N/A
2-4 years	37	44	32	N/A
Over 4 years	45	39	49	N/A
2. *Monthly EDP cost (bank's estimates)*				
Not known	35	33	35	N/A
Under $4000	33	22	39	N/A
$4000-$8000	24	34	19	N/A
Over $8000	8	11	7	N/A
3. *Number of applications on EDP*				
One only	6	0	10	N/A
2	16	6	22	N/A
3-4	41	44	39	N/A
5 or more	37	50	29	N/A
4. *Number of EDP customer services offered*				
None	8	39	78	N/A
One	14	11	16	N/A
2	14	33	3	N/A
3 or more	64	17	3	N/A
C. Other data				
Number of banks	57	18	31	8
1. *Year established*				
After 1956	14%	11%	19%	0%
1945-56	21	33	16	12
Before 1945	65	56	65	88

	Total	On-premises	Off-premises	No EDP
2. *Ownership*				
Family controlled	21	17	26	12
Less than 5 big shareholders (Over 50%)	14	28	10	0
Publicly held	46	50	35	76
Holding company	19	5	29	12
3. *Part of Country*				
Northeast (Me., Mass., Conn., N.Y., N.J., Pa.)	26%	22%	22%	50%
Southeast (Va., N.C., Tenn., Ark., Miss., Ga., Fla.)	14	17	13	12
Great Lakes (Ohio, W. Va., Wisc., Ind., Ill.)	25	11	29	38
Midwest (Minn., Kan., Mo., Tex., Okla., Colo.)	25	33	26	0
West Coast (Wash., Calif., Utah)	10	17	10	0
4. *Size of community*				
Under 10,000	12	11	16	0
10,001-40,000	39	22	42	63
40,001-100,000	23	45	13	12
100,001-250,000	9	11	3	25
Over 250,000	17	11	26	0
5. *No. of management people*				
Under 9	28	11	29	63
9-16	46	44	55	12
Over 16	26	44	16	25
6. *No. of total staff*				
Under 50	44	28	55	38
50-89	35	39	29	50
90 and more	21	33	16	12

Appendix B

Questionnaires Used

in Data Collection

(THE PITTSBURGH ADMINISTRATIVE REVIEW)

PART 7

Please answer the following informational questions concerning yourself and the nature of your job by checking the most appropriate alternative.

1. What is your sex?

26-1 ☐ male
   2 ☐ female

2. What is your age?

27-8 ☐ Under 24
   7 ☐ 24-30
   6 ☐ 31-37
   5 ☐ 38-44
   4 ☐ 45-51
   3 ☐ 52-58
   2 ☐ 59-65
   1 ☐ over 65

3. How long have you been in the banking industry?

28-6 ☐ Less than 12 months
   5 ☐ 1-2 years
   4 ☐ 3-5 years
   3 ☐ 6-10 years
   2 ☐ 11-20 years
   1 ☐ over 20 years

4. How long have you been in
   this bank?

   29-6 ⊔ Less than 12 months
      5 ⊔ 1-2 years
      4 ⊔ 3-5 years
      3 ⊔ 6-10 years
      2 ⊔ 11-20 years
      1 ⊔ over 20 years

5. How long have you been in
   your present job?

   30-5 ⊔ Less than 6 months
      4 ⊔ 7-11 months
      3 ⊔ 1-2 years
      2 ⊔ 3-5 years
      1 ⊔ over 5 years

6. In which area of the bank is your
   primary responsibility?

   31-9 ⊔ Loans
      8 ⊔ Trust
      7 ⊔ Auditing or controller
      6 ⊔ New business development
      5 ⊔ Bookkeeping
      4 ⊔ Floor operations (customer
             relations, teller, etc.)
      3 ⊔ Computer operations
      2 ⊔ Chief executive officer
      1 ⊔ Other (Please specify

   —————————————————————)

7. Major type of formal education
   beyond high school.

   33-7 ⊔ Banking
      6 ⊔ Science or Engineering
      5 ⊔ Business, Economics, or
             Accounting
      4 ⊔ Social Sciences or Liberal Arts
      3 ⊔ Computer or Systems
      2 ⊔ None
      1 ⊔ Other ————————————

PART 8

The following questions are concerned with the effects of the computer and
Electronic Data Processing (EDP) on organizational behavior. Even though
you may not consider yourself particularly knowledgeable about computers
or EDP, you are being affected either directly or indirectly by them and you
probably have some opinions regarding their effects in your bank. Please
express your frank opinion on all of the following questions, and be assured
that your responses will be held completely confidential.

1. In the next 10 to 15 years many of the decisions
   made currently by management will be made by
   the computer.   (Check one.)

   35-5 ⊔ strongly agree
      4 ⊔ agree
      3 ⊔ don't know
      2 ⊔ disagree
      1 ⊔ strongly disagree

2. The computer has enabled us to respond more
   quickly to customer needs and requests.

   36-5 ⊔ strongly agree
      4 ⊔ agree
      3 ⊔ don't know
      2 ⊔ disagree
      1 ⊔ strongly disagree

3. It is easier to give "computer people" an understanding of banking than to give "banking
   people" an understanding of the computer.

   37-5 ⊔ strongly agree
   4 ⊔ agree
   3 ⊔ don't know
   2 ⊔ disagree
   1 ⊔ strongly disagree

4. One of the biggest problems my department has
   with respect to the computer is the lack of
   available computer time for processing our work.

   38-5 ⊔ strongly agree
   4 ⊔ agree
   3 ⊔ don't know
   2 ⊔ disagree
   1 ⊔ strongly disagree

5. The computer is used in some instances to
   "control" or "supervise" performance of employees and therefore reduces the need for
   human supervision.

   39-5 ⊔ strongly agree
   4 ⊔ agree
   3 ⊔ don't know
   2 ⊔ disagree
   1 ⊔ strongly disagree

6. The utilization of computers is breaking down
   previously clear areas of functional responsibility.

   40-5 ⊔ strongly agree
   4 ⊔ agree
   3 ⊔ don't know
   2 ⊔ disagree
   1 ⊔ strongly disagree

7. People knowledgeable about the computer and
   EDP have been promoted in the bank at a faster
   rate than one would normally expect.

   41-5 ⊔ strongly agree
   4 ⊔ agree
   3 ⊔ don't know
   2 ⊔ disagree
   1 ⊔ strongly disagree

8. Bank management jobs of the future will require
   a much greater understanding of the analytic
   techniques of decision-making on the parts of the
   job occupants than is true today.

   42-5 ⊔ strongly agree
   4 ⊔ agree
   3 ⊔ don't know
   2 ⊔ disagree
   1 ⊔ strongly disagree

9. The reports I now get from the computer represent a vast improvement with regard to the
   amount and kind of information I (or someone
   in the position I now occupy) got before EDP.

   43-5 ⊔ strongly agree
   4 ⊔ agree
   3 ⊔ don't know
   2 ⊔ disagree
   1 ⊔ strongly disagree

10. In the future, people with computer knowledge
    will advance more rapidly in the bank than
    others with equal ability but no knowledge of
    computers.

    44-5 ⊔ strongly agree
    4 ⊔ agree
    3 ⊔ don't know
    2 ⊔ disagree
    1 ⊔ strongly disagree

11. Computer output is easier to understand than
    the old ledger and filing systems.

    45-5 ⊔ strongly agree
    4 ⊔ agree
    3 ⊔ don't know
    2 ⊔ disagree
    1 ⊔ strongly disagree

12. People who work directly with computers typically view the world very differently from other people in the organization.

46-5 ☐ strongly agree
4 ☐ agree
3 ☐ don't know
2 ☐ disagree
1 ☐ strongly disagree

13. In our bank we have experienced considerable frustration because computer programs were put into effect before they had been thoroughly "de-bugged" and corrected.

47-5 ☐ strongly agree
4 ☐ agree
3 ☐ don't know
2 ☐ disagree
1 ☐ strongly disagree

14. Computer reports are now being used in an optimally effective way by management.

48-5 ☐ strongly agree
4 ☐ agree
3 ☐ don't know
2 ☐ disagree
1 ☐ strongly disagree

15. "Computer people" are frequently more intrigued with what the computer can do than solving data processing problems in the best way possible.

49-5 ☐ strongly agree
4 ☐ agree
3 ☐ don't know
2 ☐ disagree
1 ☐ strongly disagree

16. In general, computers produce only standard reports which are not helpful to me in making specific decisions.

50-5 ☐ strongly agree
4 ☐ agree
3 ☐ don't know
2 ☐ disagree
1 ☐ strongly disagree

17. Banking officers and supervisors should be taught more computer know-how even though at present they may have no direct working relationship with the computer.

51-5 ☐ strongly agree
4 ☐ agree
3 ☐ don't know
2 ☐ disagree
1 ☐ strongly disagree

18. The introduction of the computer has helped to define better the actual lines of authority inside the organization.

52-5 ☐ strongly agree
4 ☐ agree
3 ☐ don't know
2 ☐ disagree
1 ☐ strongly disagree

19. Most banking officers don't know enough about computers to understand what they (computers) can do for them, so they must depend upon the computer "experts" to innovate in their area.

53-5 ☐ strongly agree
4 ☐ agree
3 ☐ don't know
2 ☐ disagree
1 ☐ strongly disagree

20. The fact that computer programs are usually
written by technical or staff people with
little or no experience in banking results in
the expenditure of a lot of energy to produce
relatively little improvement in the function
being programmed.

54-5 ☐ strongly agree
4 ☐ agree
3 ☐ don't know
2 ☐ disagree
1 ☐ strongly disagree

21. EDP has caused a certain amount of confusion
regarding the appropriate channels for the
communication of information between various levels in the organization.

55-5 ☐ strongly agree
4 ☐ agree
3 ☐ don't know
2 ☐ disagree
1 ☐ strongly disagree

22. The computer is currently playing a major
role in managerial decision-making in our
bank.

56-5 ☐ strongly agree
4 ☐ agree
3 ☐ don't know
2 ☐ disagree
1 ☐ strongly disagree

23. Computer personnel frequently bring a fresh
point of view to banking problems and consequently represent a valuable addition to
our organization.

57-5 ☐ strongly agree
4 ☐ agree
3 ☐ don't know
2 ☐ disagree
1 ☐ strongly disagree

24. In the main, computers produce reports which
are not suitable for giving personal attention
and service to individual customers.

58-5 ☐ strongly agree
4 ☐ agree
3 ☐ don't know
2 ☐ disagree
1 ☐ strongly disagree

25. Some minimum knowledge of computers and
EDP will be an absolute requirement for promotion into management ranks in the bank
within the next 10 years.

59-5 ☐ strongly agree
4 ☐ agree
3 ☐ don't know
2 ☐ disagree
1 ☐ strongly disagree

26. Younger people adjust more quickly to
changes caused by the computer.

60-5 ☐ strongly agree
4 ☐ agree
3 ☐ don't know
2 ☐ disagree
1 ☐ strongly disagree

27. The computer is essentially a big adding
machine; it is good only for accounting and
record keeping jobs.

61-5 ☐ strongly agree
4 ☐ agree
3 ☐ don't know
2 ☐ disagree
1 ☐ strongly disagree

28. Preparing input for the computer is becoming
    a time consuming job, almost equivalent
    in terms of time to the accounting work done
    prior to the computer introduction.

    62-5 ☐ strongly agree
       4 ☐ agree
       3 ☐ don't know
       2 ☐ disagree
       1 ☐ strongly disagree

29. Since the introduction of the computer, the
    need for face-to-face contact <u>between officers
    and other employees</u> of the bank for informa-
    tion exchange purposes has:

    63-3 ☐ increased
       2 ☐ decreased
       1 ☐ not changed

30. As a result of the computer and EDP, the
    amount of face-to-face contact <u>among officers</u>
    in the bank has:

    64-3 ☐ increased
       2 ☐ decreased
       1 ☐ not changed

31. Do you feel that in order for you to perform your job effectively you
    need to learn more about the computer and EDP?

    65-2 ___ Yes (Please proceed to next question.)
       1 ___ No (Please proceed to question 33.)

32. To what extent would each of the following techniques be appropriate to
    give you additional computer or EDP training? (Check one column in
    each line.)

		Very appropriate	Appropriate	Not appropriate	Don't know
		1	2	3	4
66	Periodic visits to the computer center	_____	_____	_____	_____
67	Periodic lectures or seminars in the bank	_____	_____	_____	_____
68	Short term courses (5 to 10 days) in a computer center or school	_____	_____	_____	_____
69	Long term, detailed courses (1 month) away from the bank	_____	_____	_____	_____
70	An evening course once or twice a week	_____	_____	_____	_____
71	State or national automation conventions	_____	_____	_____	_____

33. Which of the following best describes operational decision-making in your bank? (Check one line in each column.)

Before introduction of computer	After introduction of computer	
72	73	
_____	_____	1 Decisions usually made by one person alone.
_____	_____	2 Decisions usually made by one person with advice and recommendations of others.
_____	_____	3 Decisions usually made by a group of top managers.
_____	_____	4 Decisions usually made by a consensus among all managers.
_____	_____	5 No "usual" decision-making process.
_____	_____	6 I can't really say.

34. As a result of the introduction of EDP, management jobs in the bank have become: (Check one column in each line.)

		More	Less	No change associated with EDP
		1	2	3
74	Challenging	_____	_____	_____
75	Satisfying	_____	_____	_____
76	Difficult	_____	_____	_____
77	Interesting	_____	_____	_____

35. As a consequence of EDP, skill requirements in general have been upgraded, downgraded or unaffected? (Check one for each level.)

		Upgraded 3	Downgraded 2	Unaffected 1
78	Clerical level			
79	Supervisory level			
80	Management level			

36. Do you receive any output from the computer? Check one.

26-2 ___ Yes (Please proceed to next question.)
   1 ___ No (Please proceed to question 38.)

37. Please specify the nature of the output and the frequency with which you receive it.

27	Title of Report (output)	Frequency (daily, weekly, etc.)	Approximately how many hours per week do you spend reviewing each?

38. As a result of the utilization of computers, day-to-day decisions are made now at: (check one)

28-3 ☐ a higher level in the bank
   2 ☐ about the same level as before the introduction of the computer
   1 ☐ a lower level in the bank

39. The information I receive now from the computer, compared to that which I received prior to the introduction of the computer, is: (Please circle one number in each line.)

A.

Much less detailed		Less detailed		About the same		More detailed		Much more detailed
29
1	2	3	4	5	6	7	8	9

B.

Much less current		Less current		About the same		More current		Much more current
30
1	2	3	4	5	6	7	8	9

C.

Much less accurate		Less accurate		About the same		More accurate		Much more accurate
31
1	2	3	4	5	6	7	8	9

40. How do you feel the computer will affect your personal opportunities for advancement in the bank?   (Check one)

32-3 ☐ Will improve my opportunities for advancement.
   2 ☐ Will have no appreciable effect.
   1 ☐ Will make it more difficult for me to advance.

41. What has been the effect of the computer on the scope of decision-making on each of the following?   (Check as many alternatives as are appropriate for each referent.)

My subordinates:

33-1☐ increased the range of their decision-making responsibilities.

34-1☐ made their decisions more visible to others in the organization.

35-1☐ restricted the range of their decision-making responsibilities.

36-1☐ made their decisions more rational.

37-1☐ no noticeable effect.

Myself:

38-1☐ increased the range of my decision-making responsibilities.

39-1☐ made my decisions more visible to others in the organization.

40-1☐ restricted the range of my decision-making responsibilities.

41-1☐ made my decisions more rational.

42-1☐ no noticeable effect.

My "boss":

43-1☐ increased the range of his decision-making responsibilities.

44-1☐ made his decisions more visible to others in the organization.

45-1☐ restricted the range of his decision-making responsibilities.

46-1☐ made his decisions more rational.

47-1☐ no noticeable effect.

42. Below are some advantages which are often attributed to use of computers. Using the following scale please indicate for each item the extent to which you have observed the change in your bank.

Not at all		Comparatively little		To some extent		Quite a bit		A great deal
1	2	3	4	5	6	7	8	9

(You may use the same number as many times as you think appropriate. For example, if you have observed a great deal of improvement in customer service because of use of the computer, then place a "9" in the first blank space.)

48 _____ Provided better service to customers

49 _____ Provided better use of human resources

50 _____ Enabled better use of money in banks

51 _____ Opened new types of business and services

52 _____ Decreased the cost of operations

53 _____ Improved speed of operations in general

54 _____ Improved speed of data processing and bookkeeping

55 _____ Improved quality of information

56 _____ Improved accuracy of record keeping

57 _____ Made possible better management control
58 _____ Made possible better management decision-making
59 _____ Reduced the clerical workload
60 _____ Improved the image of the organization
61 _____ Created new jobs in the organization
62 _____ Other (Please specify) _____

43. Without necessarily knowing the actual facts, how do you think EDP has affected the sheer numbers of jobs in each of the following categories? (Check one alternative for each category.)

Clerical jobs (Includes Tellers)	Supervisory jobs	Managerial jobs
65-3 ☐ increased	66-3 ☐ increased	67-3 ☐ increased
2 ☐ decreased	2 ☐ decreased	2 ☐ decreased
1 ☐ no change associated with EDP	1 ☐ no change associated with EDP	1 ☐ no change associated with EDP

44. To what extent has the introduction of the computer caused any changes in the following functions of your job? (Place a check in the appropriate box in each line.)

Quite a bit 4	Somewhat 3	Not at all 2	Not applicable to my job 1		
				68	Helped in serving customers
				69	Helped to control operations
				70	Helped in the supervision of my subordinates
				71	Helped in training subordinates
				72	Increased problems of intra-organization coordination inside bank
				73	Decreased problems of intra-organization coordination inside bank
				74	Made my overall job easier

45. Below are some problems which are sometimes experienced by organizations in automating their information processing. Please estimate the extent to which you personally have observed these in your bank. Use the following scale to assign points to each item.

No problem at all		Comparatively little problem		A problem to some extent		A fairly serious problem		An extremely serious problem
1	2	3	4	5	6	7	8	9

(You may use a scale number more than once.)

26 _____ Employee resistance.
27 _____ Errors in computer output.
28 _____ Errors in preparation of material for the computer.
29 _____ Insufficient training in new procedures.
30 _____ Meeting the time deadlines for preparing computer input.
31 _____ Modifying the organization structure for more efficient informa-
32   tion flow.
33 _____ Communication between computer staff and management.
33 _____ Other (Please specify.) _____
_____
_____

46. Using the following scale, please indicate which of the following training activities you would recommend at each level. (Place one number in each space.)

Not needed at all		Only little needed		Needed to some extent		Needed, will be very useful		Essential training
1	2	3	4	5	6	7	8	9

LEVEL

Type of training	Yourself	Clerical	Supervisory	Management
Basic programming	36 _____	44 _____	52 _____	60 _____
Reading and interpreting computer output	37 _____	45 _____	53 _____	61 _____
Preparing computer input	38 _____	46 _____	54 _____	62 _____
Use of statistical analysis and mathematical tools	39 _____	47 _____	55 _____	63 _____
Capabilities of the computer	40 _____	48 _____	56 _____	64 _____
Accounting principles	41 _____	49 _____	57 _____	65 _____
Information retrieval and analysis	42 _____	50 _____	58 _____	66 _____
Model construction and utilization	43 _____	51 _____	59 _____	67 _____

47. Please indicate whether or not the computer has caused any of the following changes in the qualifications of people you need in your organization by checking one box in each line.

	Strongly agree 1	Agree 2	Don't know 3	Disagree 2	Strongly disagree 1	
68						Need more computer-oriented people
69						Need more mathematicians and quantitatively-oriented people
70						Need more marketing-oriented people
71						Need more customer contact people
72						Need more people who can make their own decisions
73						Need more people with college education
74						Need people with more knowledge in accounting
75						Need people with more analytical qualities

48. As a consequence of EDP I now spend more, less, or about the same percentage of my time:

Communicating with my "boss"

76-3 ☐ more
2 ☐ less
1 ☐ no change associated with EDP

Communicating with my subordinates

77-3 ☐ more
2 ☐ less
1 ☐ no change associated with EDP

Communicating with other officers in the bank

78-3 ☐ more
2 ☐ less
1 ☐ no change associated with EDP

Working alone

79-3 ☐ more
2 ☐ less
1 ☐ no change associated with EDP

Serving customers

80-3 ☐ more
2 ☐ less
1 ☐ no change associated with EDP

49. Are there any specific reports which you would like to receive in addition to the ones you currently get from the computer?

26-1 ___ Yes (Please specify.)
   2 ___ No

1. _____
2. _____
3. _____
4. _____

PART 3

Please estimate how much of your total working time you typically spend under average working conditions in each of the following functional activities. Write a whole number (between 0 and 100) beside each activity indicating the approximate percent of your total time spent doing your job in that activity (and the time you think you should spend). You will probably be able to make better estimates if you read the entire list of activities before responding to a particular one. Note that the total distribution of time should add up to 100 percent.

Amount of Time I Actually Spend		Amount of Time I Should Spend
	1. PLANNING: Plans include goals, strategies and courses of action. Work scheduling, budgeting, setting up procedures, setting standards, preparing agendas, and programming are all examples of planning.	
_____		_____
	2. INVESTIGATING: (Processing information): Processing information includes arranging for the collection and preparation of information, usually in the form of records, reports and accounts. Inventorying, measuring output, preparing financial reports, recordkeeping, and preparing information for the computer are common examples of managerial information processing.	
_____		_____
	3. COORDINATING: Coordinating includes exchanging information with individuals and groups within the organization in order to relate and adjust programs. Advising other departments, expediting, informing superiors, and representing one's own department in interdepartmental matters are common instances of coordinating.	
_____		_____

4. EVALUATING: Evaluating includes assessing and appraising proposals, reports and observed
performance. Employee appraisals and inspection
of actual production as well as production records,
judging financial reports, and analyzing computer
_____ output are all examples of evaluating.   _____

5. SUPERVISING: Supervising includes directing,
instructing, and leading subordinates. Counseling,
training and explaining work procedures as well as
disciplining and handling complaints are part of
_____ the supervisory function.   _____

6. NEGOTIATING: Negotiating includes repre-
senting one's organization when dealing with
individuals or groups outside the organization,
such as customers, suppliers, sales representatives,
government and civic groups, and professional
_____ associations.   _____

_____   7. Other (Please specify.) _____   _____

_____   _____

100%   _____   100%

Please estimate how much time you actually spend (and the amount of
time you think you should spend) under average working conditions consulting with or seeking information from each of the following sources of information about matters affecting your department or organization. Again, it
will be helpful to read the entire list before responding to particular items.

Amount of Time I Actually Consult With		Amount of Time I Should Consult With
_____	8. My boss.	_____
_____	9. Other persons at my same level in the organization.	_____
_____	10. My subordinates.	_____
_____	11. Statements of organizational policy.	_____
_____	12. Persons outside my organization.	_____
_____	13. Myself.	_____
_____	14. Persons above me in the organization other than my boss.	_____
_____	15. Persons below me in the organization other than my subordinates.	_____
_____	16. Other (Please specify.) _____	_____
_____	_____	_____
_____	_____	_____
100%	_____	100%

Appendix C

Major Computer Reports

Below are listed major kinds of computer-generated reports by type. The lists are not meant to be exhaustive, as many banks have initiated different versions of similar reports. The names of the reports differ from bank to bank, but we have tried to use the most descriptive titles currently in use. The specific information contained in each may also differ from bank to bank, but the kinds listed are suggestive examples of what each report is likely to include.

A. Types of Reports

    1. Demand Deposit Accounting Reports

        a. Daily Trial Balance. Lists current balance in each account, credits and debits posted the previous day, beginning balance, service charges and date of last activity. Replaces general ledger sheets. Also, provides summary information.

        b. Batch Proof Listing. Used primarily by the bookkeeping department, this is a listing of each check amount, by batch. Used for checking totals.

    c. Overdraft Report. A list of accounts with negative balance less than amount on item being processed. Includes amount overdrawn, number of days overdrawn, date of last deposit, number of times overdrawn.

    d. Stop-Hold Report. A listing of checks for which stop orders or hold orders have been received. Combined in this report is often a Float Suspect Report.

    e. Float Suspect Report. Lists pieces of information to be used as evidence of possible kiting. Examples are current balance, number and amount of debits and credits posted previous day.

    f. Significant Balance Change Report. A list of accounts for which the balance has changed the previous day by more than a specified amount or percentage of previous balance.

    g. Exceptions Report. A daily report listing all transactions which should receive attention for various bookkeeping reasons.

    h. Dormant Accounts Report. A list of accounts for which there has been no activity over a specified period of time (usually one year).

    i. Zero Balance Report. Accounts which are maintaining a zero balance, but which have not been closed.

    j. Service Charge Report. A list of accounts for which a service charge or earning has been created. Daily, weekly, or monthly depending on statement cycles.

    k. Average Balance Report. Usually printed monthly, it is a list of average balances for the last month, 6 months or year. Often part of Service Charge Report.

    l. Monthly Statement. May be full listing of all transactions, or bobtail, summarizing credits and debits. Sent to each customer on a cycle basis.

2. Time Deposit Reports

    a. Trial Balance. Balances in all accounts and changes from previous day or week.

    b. Transaction Journal. List of posted items.

    c. Interest Report. Lists interest accrued in last quarter, half and/or full year by account.

    d. W-2 Forms. Prints annual statements of interest paid to each account. Sent to customers for income tax purposes.

3. Installment Loan Reports

    a. Trial Balance. Lists current balance due, date and amount of last payment, date next payment due, rebate amount if loan closed.

    b. New Loan Journal. Lists all details of each new loan.

   c. Coupon Books. Computer-generated coupons covering all monthly payments due for the duration of the loan. Customer sends one in to the bank with each payment.

   d. Past-Due Notices. Computer prints notices to be sent to customers when delinquent 5, 10, 15 or other specified number of days.

   e. Delinquency Report. Lists all accounts on which late charges have been assessed, total late charges due, total amount of payments due and date(s) of past-due payments.

   f. Report of Transactions of Delinquents. Lists payments made on delinquent records.

   g. Aged Delinquency Report. A monthly, semi-monthly or quarterly report listing all accounts delinquent more than specified number of days.

   h. Extension Report. Lists accounts that were granted extensions.

   i. Closed Loan Journal. Lists all accounts which have been paid in full.

   j. Monthly Summary of Loans. Lists all loans outstanding, including total amount of loan, date loan was made, number and amount of payments, interest and delinquency charges, date of closing the loan.

4. General Reports

   a. Summary Report. For any computerized function, this report lists number of transactions, total debits and credits and total balances before and after day's transactions. May also list such things as number of new accounts, closed accounts, overdrafts, etc.

   b. Name and Address Report. Lists all accounts pertaining to any specified types by account number or alphabetically.

   c. Name and Address Change Report. Lists old and new name and address for specified or all accounts.

   d. New Account Report. Usually appears daily. This report lists new accounts of specified types. Often combined with Closed Account Report.

   e. Closed Account Report. Lists specified types of which have reached a zero balance and/or which have been closed by customer. Often combined with New Account Report.

   f. Rejected Items Report. Items unposted that day with coded explanation.

B. Distribution of Reports

Of the 438 respondents, 316 (72 per cent) receive at least one report on a regular basis. The percentage of officers receiving reports increases with the increase in the length of time the bank has been using EDP. While in the banks using EDP services less than two years, only 62 per cent receive output regularly; the per cent increases to 75 in the banks with over two years EDP experience. Such an increase in the number of output recipients results from two different trends. The first is the increase, over time, in the number of applications put on the computer. The second trend, which was only of minor importance in the banks visited, is the increase in the number of reports from a given application. Output is also more widely disseminated in the smaller banks (under $25 million in deposits) where there is less specialization and more need for the officers to be familiar with several applications, than in the larger ones. In the smaller banks also, the percentage of respondents receiving computer output increases to 76, compared to only 69 in the larger banks.

The number of reports a person receives varies considerably with his age. Older officers, a large percentage of whom are at higher levels of the organization, receive more reports than do the younger ones. Overall, the average number of reports received by each of the officers with regular access to output is 3.2 reports.

Index